The GIFT of GRIEF

A Practical Guide on Navigating Grief and Loss

By *Dr. M. Ajita Robinson*

Legacy Wellness Group
4915 St. Elmo Avenue Suite 506
Bethesda, MD 20876
www.legacywellnessgroup.com

Printed in the United States of America

First Printing, 2020

ISBN 978-1-7353925-0-9

Dedication

This book is dedicated to my grandfather,
Ollie Jones Jr. I am so grateful for the time we had,
your continued presence and influence.

"I listened and I listened good."

Preface

It was 2005. I finally answered the call to pivot from a career in corporate to become a mental health therapist. It would take a few more years to stop running away from doing grief and trauma work. I did everything I could to NOT be a grief therapist. Heck, I went to law school for a brief stint in between completing my master's degree and doctorate. When I stopped running and embraced the calling on my life, I found the (my) gift…and I've been abundantly blessed to bear witness and be a companion for thousands of people throughout my career and life.

The call became clear. I could not work with kids until I had done my own grief and trauma work related to my childhood. My ability to serve as a grief therapist was related to grieving my own losses, naming my own trauma.

I had not addressed my childhood trauma, so I did not feel comfortable or equipped to work with children. I could not relate to kids who experienced "normal" childhood stuff. I came to understand that part of the problem was that I did not have a tradition childhood so my lens regarding what was "normal" was skewed. I was unhealed so I could not bear witness to the journey of others because I had never experienced what it meant to be seen, heard, and protected.

Finding the gift came from serving kids like me. I could be PROOF. More importantly, I could relate to the challenges of enduring, of surviving and learning to thrive amid chaos. Finding the gift on the other side of grief allowed me to serve as a therapist, educator, and companion.

To that extent, I learned that even after loss one can find "purpose, again. A gift in grief." That despite the darkness and sheer chaos, "Joy is your birthright."

I wrote this book for the everyday person who is experiencing a variety of losses. This book is also for those who are companions on the healing journey of others.

I wrote this book for my 8-year-old self who remembers going to my great grandmother's funeral. I remember being told that grandma was just "sleeping" and being afraid to go to sleep for fear that I might not wake up. I remember kissing her cheek like I always did and my lips becoming numb and thinking I was dying. I remember no one asking if I was okay. I remember my grandmother not crying in a room full of people who were wailing in sorrow. I wrote this book for those who have lost too much and are not sure how to navigate life without…this book is for you, for me, for us.

Throughout the book, I share my knowledge in a practical way, but I also share parts of my story. Grief is a full body experience. I invite you to explore your own losses, beliefs, and experiences and have provided resources throughout the book. I have also developed a free course companion with additional resources include templates, journal prompts and videos.

Your companion with love & gratitude,

Ajita

Table of Contents

CHAPTER 1   What is Grief? 9

CHAPTER 2   Types of Losses 33

CHAPTER 3   Factors that complicate Grief 41

CHAPTER 4   Types of Grief 51

CHAPTER 5   Children and Grief 59

CHAPTER 6   Divorce and Grief 67

CHAPTER 7   Grief and the Holidays 83

CHAPTER 8   Social Media and Grief 95

CHAPTER 9   Practical Tips to Navigate Grief 105

CHAPTER 10 Cost of Making It: The Intersection
of Success and Survival 115

Grief is bourne out of deep connection and love. It is a gift. For some it is a burden that is complex and painful, for others it is an emptiness that persists. This book is intended to create a space of understanding of the universality of grief while holding true that it is a unique and individual experience that none of us escapes.

We have also created a free bonus companion course with additional resources, downloads, and short videos to help you on your journey to more fully understanding and exploring grief.

It is my sincere and heartfelt hope that you finish this practical guide having discovered the gift's that can emerge from your grief journey. As we embark on this journey, I want to remind you that grieving is a path that is often difficult to travel, but one where we can find and create meaning and restoration.

HOW TO USE THIS BOOK:

Like the grief journey, this book is written in a way that it allows you to navigate it in your own way. Each chapter is written to help you with wherever you are on this journey. I might recommend Chapter 1 and 2 as foundational so that you might fully understand where you are and what might be impacting your journey and read the others in the order that you feel led.

In this journey and in all others, take good care of you.

Dr. Ajita

Scan the QR code to register
for the course or head over to
aijtarobinson.com/thegiftofgriefresources

CHAPTER 1:
What is Grief?

Grief is the natural, normal, and necessary reaction to a loss. Though grief is a universal human experience, each loss is grieved in its own way. Grief is the process that allows us to let go of that which was and to ready ourselves for that which is to come.

It is a part of life that is repeatedly encountered and is essential to the process of becoming more fully human.

Grief is a normal human reaction to any important loss. It is a process, not an event.

Adults and children can be profoundly affected by physical and symbolic losses. I will discuss the different types of losses and factors that can impact the grieving process.

It is important for us to remember that while grief is universal, the grief journey is unique to each of us. You will hear me repeat me this a few times. It is necessary that we embrace this as truth. There is a lot of suffering that occurs because we fail to understand that others might not express grief the way that we do. We might miss the signs that others (particularly kids) are grieving. Even more, we might impact our own grief journey by holding ourselves to standards that are influenced and imposed by society. No two people journey through the grief cycle at the same pace, even when they have shared losses.

I will discuss some special and unique situations that may trigger a grief response and provide useful information to help you on your journey.

I hope that you are surrounded by people who love and support you. I also hope that you give yourself permission to be where you are on your journey. Grief is a life-long journey, one that never ends for most of us… at best, we adjust and find new ways to carry the weight.

It is important to note that this book does not replace going to therapy.

Our grief journey is largely impacted by our ability to identify and name our losses. Western cultures often avoid discussing grief as a part of life. We often limit the discussion to death related losses. In a way, this primes us towards denying and dismissing the losses we encounter on a regular basis. This denies the notion that grief is a normal and natural part of living and not a response to limited to death and dying.

We would be better prepared to name, process and heal from the cumulative losses we experience such as loss of relationships, dreams, jobs, homes, friends, expectations, safety and more.

This book is intended to provide an overview of grief and loss and some practical information to help parents, caregivers, educators, and clinicians who are navigating grief or bearing witness to the journey of others. It is also written to help us claim healing by becoming more fully aware of our losses so that we might find the grief is life post loss.

HOW DO YOU DEFINE GRIEF?

Grief is defined as a set of feelings, thoughts and behaviors that are triggered when a person is faced with loss or the threat of loss.

How can it be differentiated from worry, stress, or sadness?

Worry, stress and sadness can all be a part of the grief journey. The difference with grief is the trigger is related to loss. The way we handle sadness, stress, and worry that are a result of grief is different than how we might approach stress that is due to workplace stress, relationship, environmental or social stressors.

WHAT ARE THE STAGES OF GRIEF?

The stage or process models of grief originally purported by Elizabeth Kubler-Ross and others have long sense been debunked and revised. Kubler-Ross herself moved away from the stages model of grief. Stages tend to imply that the grief journey is a linear process when we have learned that it is not and to treat it as such could create additional harm to the bereaved.

Instead of grief being a linear, stage or phase approach we know understand that it is a process or journey.

The journey below in a combination of theories set forth by major grief theories and this authors' contribution to the journey.

THE JOURNEY THROUGH GRIEF: THE GIFT OF GRIEF MODEL

The Gift of Grief model sets forth 9 universal truths related to grief and finding the gift in any loss.

I.   Recognizing the reality of the loss is necessary part of the grieving process.

II.   Grief is a survival mechanism.

III. There is no one way to grieve.

IV.   Grief is cumulative even in single incident losses because of primary and secondary losses.

V.   Grieving does not prevent us from also living in the present moment.

VI.   We grief in anticipation of loss and when they occur

VII. Grief is a lifelong journey, unanchored by time

VIII. Grief goal is not to resolve the loss but to create life post loss

IX.   Finding the gift in grief requires that we accept that we have purpose after loss

Grief theorists agree on the following components of the grief journey

- Recognizing the reality of the loss: knowing and understanding that the loss occurred whether it is a physical or symbolic loss

- Expressing feelings/emotions associated with the loss. There will be a wide range and depth of emotions: some expected, some not

- Organizing and adjusting to a changed life (coping, making changes, ascribing new roles and slowing moving forward/exploring a new reality)

- Relocating the lost love from a physical presence in our outer world to a perpetual place in our inner world. Learning to live with and appreciate our memories

- Gaining new perspectives, re-establishing and re-discovering a future which had been challenged by the loss. Finding hope, faith, and renewed meaning. We also want to make special that there is no right way of navigating through this process. We might find ourselves cycling through different aspects of acceptance, gaining new perspective, etc at different times throughout our healing process.

Grieving doesn't always follow a set schedule.

- Grief can be delayed

- Grief can be recurring

- Certain events or memories may trigger the unfinished grief process

- Current grieving may also trigger unfinished grief from the past

- It can take well over a year to get through grieving process

People can go through several aspects of the grief cycle at once and experience different levels of peace or distress. The single biggest myth related to grief is that it just takes time. Time alone doesn't heal the pain of grief. Grief is a holistic experience involving physical, emotional, and psychological processes. It is important that we honor that our grief journey may be lighter at times and heavier at other points.

We find that people who are able to find a way to accept the reality of the loss and find meaning post loss often find meaning in sharing their story, accessing their support system, and giving themselves time to feel the full range of emotions that accompanies grief.

A variety of factors can impact the grieving process including: one's loss history (grief can be cumulative), the relationship of the deceased, how one learned about the loss, whether the loss was due to natural causes or not, and so on. We will discuss this more in the next section.

How long does the grieving process usually last? What factors might cause this to differ? What can make grieving easier or harder?

Grieving does not follow a set schedule. Grief can be delayed. In the face of loss, we often get busy with the tasks of burial, moving, reorganizing life and thus the journey of grief gets delayed. Grief can also be a recurring process that is triggered by unfinished grief, anniversaries, holidays, and new losses. Grief is not anchored by time.

Give yourself permission to grieve:

- **Don't fight your feelings** – It's normal to have lots of ups and downs, and feel many conflicting emotions, including anger, resentment, sadness, relief, fear, and confusion. It's important to identify and acknowledge these feelings. While these emotions will often be painful, trying to suppress or ignore them will only prolong the grieving process.

- **Talk about how you're feeling** – Even if it is difficult for you to talk about your feelings with other people, it is very important to find a way to do so when you are grieving. Knowing that others are aware of your feelings will make you feel less alone with your pain and will help you heal. Journaling can also be a helpful outlet for your feelings.

- **Remember that moving on is the end goal** – Expressing your feelings will liberate you in a way, but it is important not to dwell on the negative feelings or to over-analyze the situation. Getting stuck in hurtful feelings like blame, anger, and resentment will rob you of valuable energy and prevent you from healing and moving forward.

- **Remind yourself that you still have a future** – When you commit to another person, you create many hopes and dreams. It's hard to let these dreams go. As you grieve the loss of the future you once envisioned, be encouraged by the fact that new hopes and dreams will eventually replace your old ones.

- **Know the difference between a normal reaction to a breakup and depression** - Grief can be paralyzing after a breakup, but after a while, the sadness begins to lift. Day by day, and little by little, you start moving on. However, if you don't feel any forward momentum, you may be suffering from depression.

WHAT IS THE GIFT OF GRIEF?

"People who are grieving, do not need fixing. They need compassion. They need companions." - Dr. Ajita Robinson

They need space to experience rather than be moved to different ways of feeling and being. They need space that is free of goals and expectations, benchmarks, and achievements. The bereaved is the expert in their grief journey. When doing our own grief work and bearing witness to the grief of others we want to be mindful of the expectations that we might have of ourselves and others. Even when we are grieving a shared loss, our grief journey is unique to each of us.

This journey creates an opportunity for each of us to find the gift in one's grief journey and integrate ones losses by acknowledging their impact on our present moment, observing them and allowing these gifts to show up on our journey through navigating life post loss.

Being a companion as our loved ones navigate their own grief journey often include rituals, honoring, activities, being trusted stewards of the narrative and stories, our loved ones need to share and other bearing-witness opportunities that accompany grief.

The Gift of Grief is about bearing witness to the spiritual connection that remains, even after a physical tie has been severed. It is about feeling our feelings, acknowledging the wholeness, the sadness, the joy. It is about focusing on being and not doing. It is about allowing ourselves to learn from our lived experience, from our sorrows, from our joy, from our pain and from others. It is about giving ourselves permission to be exactly where we are. Without movement, without noise, without words, and without judgment.

When we embrace the gift that grief brings, we might allow ourselves to create a space of silence from outside voices, from outside expectations, from external struggles and be present in a way that allows us to heal.

That is a gift that we give ourselves in the aftermath of loss. This creates a space for anyone helping, healing, or witnessing to listen with new ears and new ways of being with curiosity versus concern. To create safety amid suffering and chaos.

To recognize the organization and prioritization of tasks serves as a way of making meaning, of that which is no more that we also create a way of understanding that highlights the strengths, and what's working, even in the midst of a disaster that we are adopt a stance of compassion.

We come to realize and accept that loss is a natural part of life. It is not the end or the beginning. It is simply a part of the journey. For many, grief creates a new lens to view the world and one's purpose in life. We might honor our loss by living more fully, cherishing the present and letting go of control of the past and future. We might be moved to start new traditions, routines, and causes. These are all gifts that harvest after loss.

At the core of grief work requires that:

We focus on the reality of the loss and focus on life's (new) meaning.

We often focus on helping the grieving person access positive family and social support in the face of loss.

We are tasked with helping the grieving person become self-compassionate as they navigate the difficult aspects of the grief journey.

We want to remove the stigma and myth related to time and the grief process. We want to embrace that grief spikes continue for life through events, holidays, "anniversaries", milestones and life events.

We seek to create honoring rituals and practices that allow for positive and adaptive expressions of grief.

"Grief is a full body experience." – Dr. Ajita M. Robinson

As I approached the anniversary of a loss, I would begin to feel sick. I mean full on flu-like symptoms. The first Thanksgiving that I spent back home after both my grandfather and brothers passing landed me in the hospital. They could not quite figure out what was wrong, so I was treated for a virus. I was severely dehydrated, gastrointestinal issues, nausea, you name it. All the screening came back clear. This pattern repeated every year, every anniversary, holiday, and milestone for nearly two years. Grief impacts the whole person. We must learn to recognize how it shows up in our body.

Physical, Behavioral, Cognitive and Special response to loss

There are so many ways that loss affects us. Every dimension of our being, both as individuals, and collectively are impacted by grief.

Some of the things that we discuss below might be amplified. It might feel intense and disproportionate depending on whether the loss was sudden, violent, or otherwise ambiguous.

Our ability to reconcile our grief experience depends on a lot of contributing factors that might be happening in our individual and collective life. We might explore: What is happening in our world? What resources, internal and external, do we have at our disposal?

Grief is not an isolated event that happens, it happens amid life with existing stressors that do not alleviate in the face of loss.

This following list is not exhaustive, nor is it all encompassing. It does not apply to everyone. Grief is a universal experience and individual journey. Our reactions might be different, our experiences and expression of grief might change over time, allow that to naturally flow. What is presented below are common physical, behavioral, and cognitive responses to grief and loss.

Physical reactions. Our physical response to grief is one way of handling the stress, anxiety, overwhelm and disbelief, that comes with loss. The body often exhibits grief symptoms well before we are 1) conscious of the experience and 2) able to name the response as grief.

Some possible physical reactions include:

Changes in our appetite. We might notice that we have lost our appetite, that we are under eating or we are overeating. Some people binge eat. Our relationship and appetite with food can be temporarily altered in response to a loss. Although, we expect it to be a temporary change, we want to be mindful about any swift changes in either direction, overeating, binge eating, deprivation and starvation.

It is normal that we might not have an appetite, or we might use food as coping mechanism. It is important that we do not evaluate it too negatively unless it does not return to pre-loss patterns. In the immediate aftermath of grief, we might give ourselves permission to observe the change in our appetite and the desires of our body.

Food is nourishment even when we do not have a taste for our favorite meal or normal comfort foods. It is important to remember to give your body some of the nutrients it needs, so that you have the internal resources to do the task of grief.

Sleep. We might also notice that our sleep is disrupted, or our sleep patterns have changed. Changes in sleep might include oversleeping, difficulty falling asleep, or staying asleep. Our sleep quality could be impacted. We might notice that we slept for the requisite numbers of hours but are still waking up feeling exhausted and depleted. Excessive sleeping might provide a break from our reality. We might experience nightmares and interrupted sleep, daydreaming and sleep that is loss centered.

Lack of Motivation or energy. It is common for grieving people to experience a loss of motivation or loss of energy. These changes are normal when navigating a loss.

There are other physical responses to grief that might show up that can exacerbate existing physical challenges or demands on our body.

We might notice changes in our blood pressure, whether it is elevated or low (hypertension or hypotensive, respectively).

Difficulties controlling diabetes and our glucose levels.

We might notice difficulty managing our allergies, digestive and stomach pains, and other Gastrointestinal problems. Headaches, migraines, muscle fatigue are also commonly reported symptoms.

All of these can be exacerbated when we are under nourished and dehydrated and when we are fatigued. The body's immune system is responding to the stress and strain that accompanies loss.

It is important that we continue to engage in nurturing of our physical body to maintain our immune system and our ability to remain healthy. There is correlational data and evidence that grief can often manifest with physical symptomology such as cold and flu like symptoms. The body is more vulnerable to illness and disease during times of stress.

Even when it feels like another thing that we do not have motivation to do, your body and your grief journey will thank you for engaging in restorative self-care.

Behavioral responses to grief.

There are some behavioral responses that may show up in the face of loss that might change individual behaviors when we are alone or in social settings.

We might observe more aggressive behaviors. This may be evidenced by pressured speech and tone, volume, irritability and tension in our communication, our body and evidenced by our behavior. We might also retreat, withdraw, or become noticeably quiet and turn inward. This turning inward is not the same as what we see when one is being self-reflective, but in a way that creates distance between our self and others. We might also find ourselves or our loved ones to be rather short with answers, unable to engage in lengthy conversation and feeling unworthy. They might demonstrate an inability to express a range of emotions such as happiness, joy, sadness, and laughter. It is a reminder that these feelings are natural and normal in the immediate aftermath of grief. Joy, happiness, and laughter can sit alongside grief, sorrow and loss. For some people, experiencing joy during the midst of grief feels dishonoring to their loved one or it may feel forced or inappropriate.

We might experience self-doubt and guilt.

When my grandfather was in the hospital, I remember receiving the update from his medical team that despite aggressively treating the pneumonia, he wasn't getting better. He was, in fact, rapidly deteriorating. The pneumonia was exacerbated by lung cancer that had caused part of his lung to collapse. I remember feeling guilty for not knowing that he was sick and for not coming home sooner. I recall replaying all the medical decisions, consulting with every specialist I could find. My grandfather had an advanced directive that laid out very clearly that circumstances upon which life support should be removed. Although, I knew I would carry out his wishes I was riddle with doubt regarding whether I was making the right decision or giving him enough time to fight. After discussing with my immediate family and his siblings, we decided that we would remove support on Friday at noon. That would give all of the family members and opportunity to come in town and say their final goodbyes. On Friday morning at 7:02 a.m. the ICU nurse called my cellphone and advised me that my grandfather had died.

We may question whether we had done enough, we might question our decisions in those final moments, or hours. We may need reassurance even when we cannot quite accept it. We might have a global sense of meaningless and hopelessness. Even when we want to engage in activities, it might be difficult to check in, it might be difficult to engage, it might be difficult to just leave the comfort and familiarity of our home.

Grievers are prone to engaging in reckless, or self-destructive behaviors that include:

- alcohol use

- drug use

- sexual promiscuity

- reckless driving gambling

- and other risk-seeking behaviors

These behaviors can detrimental to one's emotional, financial, spiritual, and psychological well-being. The goal of these behaviors aren't to self-destruct but rather to cope with the pain and life post loss.

Self-destructive behaviors are often aimed at numbing the pain, numbing the feelings, and escaping from the overwhelming emotional response and the burden of life post loss. It is important to note that these behaviors are often seeking of comfort, to seek feeling in a world that feels void of meaning, hope and love and are often ways to maintain or regain control.

In a world that feels so unpredictable hyperactivity is another common response to grief, especially in males.

This may present as excessive energy. It may be a need to do "something". The purpose might be to serve and to have meaning, relieve stress and anxiety and find purpose. Being still for many people is too heavy to bear.

Hyperactivity might include:

- Excessive cleaning

- Immediately returning to work

- Excessive talking in a way that doesn't leave room for one's inner thoughts that doesn't leave room for one to find and explore their authentic feelings and experiences in the loss.

- Shopping

- Gambling

- Excessive organizing

- Starting projects are never finished.

- Spending beyond what is reasonable, feasible or comfortable

- Engaging in attention getting and attention seeking behaviors in ways that are outside of the normal way of being or pre-loss behavior for the person again it is.

These responses exist on a continuum. Whether they are normal is relative to the individual's pre-loss state, their pre-crisis way of being and the disruption of daily functioning. They are not to be compared with anyone else's way of being, experiencing or responding to grief. We should be careful to not over pathologize normal reactions or responses to loss

COGNITIVE REACTIONS TO GRIEF

Cognitive reactions include reduced attention span, an inability to follow conversations, difficulty staying on task or inability to follow or stay engaged in conversation. Cognitive reactions also include challenges with staying in the present moment. These difficulties might impact their job performance, caregiving responsibilities, and increased forgetfulness. Cognitive responses might also include loss centered thinking to the exclusion of other thought processes, loss-centered thought that interfere with present and future oriented thoughts. Grievers may experience or notice an impaired sense of self-esteem, idealization of the past or the future, an idealization of the person or relationship lost. It is common in many societies to not speak ill of the dead, or to speak poorly of a past partner, as it is often viewed as taboo. Idealization of the person can set in as a coping mechanism, and socialized way of communicating about the deceased. The absence of being able to reconcile the reality of the relationship with the person might interfere with the grief process and may contribute to disenfranchised or complicated grief.

Engaging in Magical Thinking might occur when all reasonable and realistic evidence points an outcome being impossible. Magical thinking should not be equated to beliefs related to supernatural power and intervention that many who ascribe to faith based and religious beliefs encounter and experience as truth in their own life. Reactions to loss might also include blaming oneself, excessive guilt, or statements such as "I could have", "I should have", or "I should not have", "If only I had", etc. Feeling blame, guilt and regret are common responses to loss.

On the other side of shame and guilt might be feelings of hopelessness and helplessness. Feeling a loss of power to intervene or to change the outcome is prevalent among grievers. Many people experience fear of being alone, of being a single parent of being single and of being forgotten.

Many grievers express fear of the thought of forgetting the sound of a loved one's voice, the sound of their laughter, the fear that they will simply lose their memories with that person or that period in their life.

There is also fear and guilt when one begins to adjust to life post loss that can feel dishonoring for some people. This can be particularly difficult for people who have survived traumatic and violent circumstances.

We might have fears around whether we have made the right decision to end a relationship, to terminate life support, to leave a job or whatever the life transition may be.

Many people also experience fear of the unknown: not knowing what might happen next, what decisions they will have to make on their own, or what journey lies ahead. Fear can be immobilizing.

Anger is a part of the grief journey.

In the face of life circumstances, we might find ourselves angry at God, angry at the unfairness, angry at others for the ways that they have let us down, the ways that they have contributed to our loved ones suffering. We might even find ourselves angry at our loved one for not telling us, for not letting us be present, for not fighting, for leaving us to face life without them. Underneath anger is often sadness, fear, shame, helplessness, and sorrow. As previously mentioned, anger is often more readily accessible, more easily recognized, and it feels safe, but it is not the work of reconciliation on the grief journey. It is not the work of healing. We might find ourselves yearning, desiring the lost loved one, and the world that we enjoyed, that we knew before the loss. We might struggle with creating a life for our self for our children, and secondary losses might manifest because of the primary loss.

ANXIETY AND GRIEF GO HAND IN HAND

All the things that we have discussed can create an accumulation of general anxiety for many individuals who are struggling with grief. Many people find themselves overwhelmed with life and with all the responsibility of making decisions on their own, of creating a new normal. We might find ourselves anxious about all the changes, the newness. Until we find ways to hold grief in our arms and develop the muscle memory for carrying it, that does not leave us fatigued, we might feel anxious, angry, and overwhelmed.

SPIRITUAL AND PHILOSOPHICAL RESPONSES TO GRIEF

Whatever one's belief system might be, grief often challenges that system. What we believed might come into question in the face of loss. We might examine how our beliefs fit considering this current loss, especially when it feels unimaginable. When it is unpredictable, and tragic. How do we reconcile our spiritual and religious thoughts that God is all knowing that God is all powerful that God is able, and yet… *"in my time of need, God didn't intervene"*? We might feel abandoned, feel unheard and these experiences, these unanswered prayers might leave us questioning our beliefs. One's anger and disappointment towards God might cause one to question their faith or previously held beliefs.

One's spiritual responses may include a loss of meaning in the world, a loss of acceptance over what life looks like post loss, a loss of connection to all that felt whole, real, and good.

One's grief and mourning involve a variety of life transitions and changes. It requires that we engage in a process of reconciliation and adaptation, that is not to be confused with forgiving, getting over, moving on. As we seek support, encouragement and guidance on this journey we might question, and evaluate our existing coping mechanisms, our internal and external resources, our sense of community in relation to the world, our spiritual and philosophical beliefs and resent the tasks required to find the gift in life post loss.

When we experience a loss, we begin to navigate the grief process.

Mourning are the actions, behaviors, and tasks that we can see, whereas grief is an internal process experienced by the grieving person. Rituals in general are defined as a symbolic activity that is performed before, during or after a meaningful event in order to achieve some desired outcome- rituals can range from activities designed to alleviate grief to one's bedtime routine.

Rituals can be powerful in helping one cope with loss and to establish new habits, feelings and behaviors. In terms of loss, rituals give us an opportunity to "do" something with our feelings. In terms of funerals and rites, these rituals give us a socially acceptable space to express, engage, honor and hold our grief. Rituals allows us to have shared experiences and memory making with those who are also grieving.

Funerals, rites, cleansing rituals, preparing the burial clothing and adornments and other mourning rituals are our last opportunity to take care of our loved ones in the physical sense. In some cultures, rituals are aligned with religious and spiritual beliefs regarding preparing their loved one for their next life.

Rituals can provide a sense of comfort and containment during our grief journey. Unlike the actual loss, which can often be unexpected and shocking, we usually know what is expected during a ritual. Amid chaos, rituals can ground us in the comfort of familiarity. Rituals can help restore a sense of control, a sense of belonging and connectedness.

Rituals are made up of actions that represent ideas, thoughts, myths or beliefs. This creates room for us to create new rituals that honor the ideas and beliefs we have about the deceased or the symbolic losses we are mourning.

There are so many rituals that exist and that we can create. It's important that we find ways to identify what we need and to give ourselves permission to be creative, nonjudgmental and compassionate as we engage in activities during our healing journey. It is okay to try new things, even when we learn that they do not work as expected in certain situations.

Many of these rituals are family and community centered practices. We don't often think of them in terms of entertainment but rather are designed as ways to honor the deceased and create community for those grieving.

Many rituals are intended to pay respects to the deceased as well as the surviving family. Some rituals are grounded in spiritual and religious beliefs and practices. It is important that we understand that these rituals should be viewed as ways of honoring and it's important that we create a stance of curiosity and respect even when a ritual might conflict with our own beliefs and grief style.

Chapter 9 discusses in more detail rituals and ways to navigate the loss journey.

Dying persons are living… some are dying more actively than others.

Dying is the natural process that leads to death. Dying, however, is not the culmination of one's life.

Cultural factors that impact death and dying include but are not limited to religious beliefs, social, spiritual, economic, and other meaningful sources of influence. These factors can be present on a micro (individual) or macro (societal/systemic) level. These factors may be explicit or implicit in the impact on how they shape a persons' perspective and responses regarding death and dying.

Thus, it is important to understand the cultural beliefs, values, rituals and norms and the differences in these factors to fully understand one's relationship to death and dying. A fuller understanding of these factors can help us understand ourselves and others with an informed and holistic view.

Our religious beliefs, values, attitudes and acceptance or rejection of these influences serve as a benchmark that can define our behavior, feelings, thoughts and practices during the dying, death, and grief journey.

Observed rituals and stated beliefs can be distinguished between different religious groups (e.g. Christian sects, Islamic groups, Buddhism, Hinduism, etc). It is easy to fall prey to stereotypical beliefs about other religious and cultural practices. It is important that we honor the differences in beliefs, values, and practices as valuable to the member of their distinct cultural groups. We should remain self-aware and actively engaged in introspective regarding our implicit bias and work to educate ourselves and eradicate thoughts and feelings that are not sensitive, accurate or promotive to the cultural norms of others.

It would be a disservice to attempt to cover the various religious, spiritual beliefs, practices, values, and rituals that exist. Therefore, we will put forth the following guiding principles to create an informed, open dialogue of respect and curiosity.

We grieve in advance, before the loss occurs. When we are aware, ahead of time, that an end is imminent, we begin to grieve. This is anticipatory grief. We might be preparing for the death of a loved one or the end of a relationship that has run its course. We grieve that change in jobs or income. Many students grieve when they change schools, even when it is a good change such as graduating from middle school to high school. We anticipate the change in a relationship after a disagreement or confrontation. The anticipatory grief process can also be filled with significant anxiety. This process does not prevent us from navigating grief when the loss actually occurs.

Resource on the portal: Helping your explore grief guided exploration

Did you receive a nugget that helped you? Share with me if you feel moved at thegift@ajitarobinson.com

NOTES:

CHAPTER 2:
Types of Losses

Understanding loss and factors that impact the grief process

Grief can occur for a variety of reasons. The grief journey is often created as a result of two broad categories of loss: physical losses and symbolic losses.

It's important that we recognize that a loss is defined by the griever. Sometimes we have difficulty naming our grief or aren't consciously aware that the changes in our body, emotional and psychological state is related to a loss.

Physical losses are more readily recognizable and often honored by society with rituals, and other socially recognized mourning practices. Physical loss is generally marked by the physical loss of a person, animal, or body part.

Examples of physical losses

Physical separation from a loved one who moves away, is kidnapped, or ends a relationship. The loss of connection when reconnection is not possible triggers a loss response.

The death of a loved one triggers the grief response. When a loved one dies, we grieve. We navigate a journey that is not linear and often painful. Grief of a loved one is a lifelong journey.

Symbolic losses are non-physical and may be things such as a divorce, or job loss, or loss of one's identity or mobility to name a few.

Loss is experienced anytime we lose something that we had become attached to and it is no longer there or available.

Physical losses can also occur when we lose something tangible of value (monetary or sentimental). We might grieve the physical loss of our home due to fire, destruction or financial ruin.

Our memories and emotional connection to spaces and things are real and the loss of this connection can cause mourning.

We could also lose our physical health and mobility due to an accident, violence or chronic illness.

My grandmother suffered 7 mini strokes in a single day resulting in paralysis (below the waist). The paralysis led to her becoming bed bound. Individuals who are bed bound are at increased risk for developing bed sores and circulatory issues. Despite 24-hour care, Occupational therapy and Physical therapy, my grandmother developed arterial blockage that cut off circulation to the lower half of her leg resulting in an above knee amputation. In addition to grieving the loss of her mobility and limb, she also grieved the loss of identity. Prior to suffering 7 strokes and the subsequent medical issues, she was the matriarch of 18 siblings and primary homemaker and caregiver for her husband. The strokes switched her role and identity from caregiver to the one receiving care.

Examples of symbolic losses:

Grieving the loss of the relationship (divorce, break up, separation, etc), companionship, and shared experiences. We encounter loss of relationships when we "outgrow" friendships or intimate partnerships. Many people grieve relationship they have with their parents, siblings or family members. We may not recognize these as losses. Grief often manifest because of disappointment, rejection and unmet needs we have versus the relationship we might have needed, desired or expected.

Many people grieve the loss of relationships with parents who are physically present but emotionally unavailable. One might describe having to grieve a parent who is not the person they grew up knowing and loving. One might grieve the loss of an open and trusting relationship with a parent that has breached the trust in the relationship because of theft related to addiction, gambling, and cocaine. Additionally, I have worked with clients who have had to navigate grieving the death of a parent they never knew. These individuals would likely grieve the loss of the relationship they hoped for as well as the loss of future hopes of having a relationship.

Loss of support, be it financial, intellectual, emotional, or social.
As a first-generation college student, I found myself grieving the loss of support, stability, and the loss of a trusted "guide." Although, my family was proud of me for having made it to college, there was no one who had done it before me so there were so many gaps in knowledge, and avoidable mistakes were made as a result of this gap. My family didn't know how to support me and I was in the thick of survival and didn't quite know what I needed. The coronavirus, a public health crisis caused by a respiratory disease, has created collective loss of socialization, community, loss of normality, income, identity and interrupted milestones for many due to prolonged physical distancing and the risk factors associated with this illness. In Chapter 9, we discuss specific ways grief is impacted by distance and how to navigate these circumstances.

Loss of hopes, plans, and dreams (can be even more painful than practical losses). Loss of hope shows up in a variety of ways. We might struggle with feeling hopeless that we might ever recover after the death of a child or spouse. We might lose hope of finding a companion or partner who loves us the way we want to be loved. We might feel a loss of hope and dreams following a divorce or separation.

Loss of a home, a job, identity (retirement, mobility, caregiving), etc. We might grieve the loss of our identity when we retire or experience an injury that changes our identity. Many people have lost a child struggle with whether they are still a "parent" if their child has died.

Loss of health due to chronic or terminal illness. Many of us take our health for granted until it is negatively impacted or compromised. Many new parents whose children are born with illness or different abilities grieve the loss of dreams or plans they had for the life they planned for their child or the life their child may have enjoyed if not born with a chronic illness of other abilities.

Loss of safety (emotionally, physical, and psychological). Loss of safety can be described a physical such as in the cases of physical abuse or neglect. Safety can also refer to emotional and psychological needs. It is important to remember that the individual defines safe and unsafe.

Children and individuals in inner city communities riddled with poverty, violence, housing and food insecurity might grieve the loss of stability and safety. Often times public health professionals discuss factors that impact obesity and other health outcomes for minority youth but neglect to address the societal and environmental factors that such as police brutality, and neighborhood violence that are contributing factors that better explain decrease exercise and physical activity among these individuals. Additionally, many inner-city communities lack appropriate food sources such as grocery stores and farmers markets, another factor that impacts health outcomes. Individuals in these communities might also grieve the systemic factors that contribute to a global loss of safety, stability, and opportunity.

In relation to loss of safety, marginalized communities grieve being Black and Indigenous People of Color in environments that are often oppressive and unsafe because of anti-Black, systemic, institutional and historical policies, systems and societal norms. The loss of humanity, safety and stability can compound the grief process for these individuals. Individuals from marginalized communities are more likely to experience cumulative losses, limited access to adequate and culturally responsive care and disparate healthcare outcomes. Additionally, individuals from marginalized communities are more likely to experience traumatic exposures and thus more likely to develop and exhibit symptoms of traumatic grief.

We rarely experience loss in isolation. Our life stressors continue, and new losses often have a compounding effect. Most losses have both a primary loss and a secondary loss. A primary loss is usually the originating event of loss. A secondary loss occurs because of the primary loss.

The primary loss might be the death of a parent. A secondary loss might include physical and symbolic losses such as loss of income, loss of identity, loss of a home and more. These losses also trigger a grief response and can complicate the grief process.

Resource on the portal: Loss History activity

Did you receive a nugget that helped you? Share with me if you feel moved at thegift@ajitarobinson.com

Resource on the portal: Loss History activity

Did you receive a nugget that helped you? Share with me if you feel moved at thegift@ajitarobinson.com

NOTES:

CHAPTER 3:
Factors that Complicate Grief

The grieving process can be triggered and impacted by a variety of factors. We will cover a few of the common ones that we see occur in our work with individuals, children, and families.

In terms of physical losses, **one's relationship to the deceased** can impact how the bereaved navigates the grief process. The closer and more connected the relationship the more difficult the process might be. This isn't meant to quantify or qualify relationships and losses but rather to highlight that the closer the relationship the impact of the loss is likely to impact multiple areas of the bereaved person's life. For example losing a spouse or a child losing a parent is likely to have a more profound impact on the daily life of the bereaved than the loss of a distant relative. However, the absence of a relationship or a complicated relationship with the deceased can also have a profound impact.

For example, a young woman's father died was debating whether to attend the funeral. The daughter was born from an extramarital affair. The woman grieved the death of her father, a man she didn't know, the loss of a future relationship with him, the loss of relationships with her siblings, and the loss associated with not being recognized as a griever (disenfranchised grief) and the loss of support usually provided to those who have lost a parent.

How the deceased died and how the loved ones found out. My grandfather died after being in the hospital for 10 days. He was 70 years old and died of pneumonia that was exacerbated by lung cancer. He smoked for 58 years. While his death had an impact on our family, we were able to make meaning around him having lived a long and good life and died of natural consequences of being a lifelong smoker and having refused chemo. He died on his own terms.

In contrast, my oldest brother died the following June. A young and vibrant man in his early 40's. He died in a swimming pool accident. We were completely shocked and unprepared to lose him so early in his life. My brothers' death was complicated for a variety of reasons. He died in another state and it took months for us to get the autopsy report back to confirm how we died. One of my siblings and some of my extended family **found out about his death** via social media which wasn't the ideal circumstances to receive such difficult news.

Other factors that can impact the grieving process is the **developmental stage** and cognitive capacity of the bereaved. We will spend some time discussing how grief is different for children. It is outside of the scope of this book to discuss how those who are neurotypical might have difficulties processing death and grief. I will share that my brother's oldest daughter, who was his next of kin, has severe autism. We were concerned with whether she understood the finality of death and were faced with having to show that his son (second oldest child) was effective next of kin because my niece due to cognitive limitations was unable to consent to release the body or make decisions. We were fortunate to have documents in place to allow our family to decide and act on my nephew's behalf in making funeral arrangements for my unmarried brother.

The bereaved persons loss history. The cumulative history of losses can impact one's grief journey. Some of us have had a series of losses that are unhealed and unresolved that can accumulate and create complex grief and trauma for the bereaved.

Mental health status of the bereaved at the time of loss. The overall wellness, including mental wellness, of the bereaved can impact their ability to cope with a physical or symbolic loss. If one is already overwhelmed your ability to handle another blow might be diminished because we may not have enough mental and emotional resources to rally. Under these circumstances the bereaved can experience what is often discussed as a psychological or mental breakdown.

An existing support system. When the griever has an accessible, healthy support system they tend to fare better as they have sources of support during this vulnerable time. They are less likely to be isolated and alone. They are more likely to have friends and family to ensure that the have basic needs and socialization which can serve as a protective factor against complex grief.

Relationship not sanctioned or recognized. The relationship of the bereaved and deceased may complicate the grieving process. This occurs in a variety of circumstances, most commonly in same-sex relationships. However, there are a variety of grievers that go unrecognized because they are simply missed as being affected.

Relationship status and/or relationship quality might impact the grief process. Positive affectional bonds or secure attachments between loved ones, children and parent, one adult to another human in connection with one another, can result in a grief experience or response that is both natural, normal and adaptive for continued life live post loss.

However, when they are unhealthy, or insecure attachments, one might experience numbing, complicated grief, disorganization, and complicated responses that change the way one can yearn and mourn and express their grief.

When there is a painful or abusive relationship between the deceased and the bereaved this can also impact the grief journey. This is common among those who have endured child sexual abuse or childhood trauma and their abuser is a family member or caregiver. The bereaved person might have sorry, sadness AND feelings of relief. They might be "safe" for the first time and finally be free from the painful relationship and experience guilt because of feeling relieved.

It is important that individuals can navigate a process of healing, where they are able to accept the finality of death related losses.

The inability to accept the finality and the permanence of death is an indicator that grief may be chronic or conflicted and would require further professional support from a grief and trauma trained expert.

If the griever is not recognized. In our work in the community, particularly in schools impacted by violence, we most often see the school counselors and educators fall in the category of not being recognized as griever. When was the last time you saw a grief support group for teachers whose students who died? It's unheard of. These educators and counselors spend a significant amount of time without kids, yet they are forgotten about during times of grief. They are impacted and often unsupported and unrecognized as grievers.

Religious beliefs/traditions. What one believes about what happens to the deceased after death might impact the grief journey. We often have parents contact us because they aren't sure how to explain their beliefs about death and dying, as it relates to their faith or absence of faith, to their children. For example, individuals who believe in an after-life or reincarnation may experience some solace in knowing that they may be reunited with their loved one.

Poverty/Finances. This one is often overlooked or missed by those not impacted by poverty or limited finances. In my work at the county morgue, I routinely encountered families from economically disadvantaged backgrounds who in addition to grieving the loss of their loved one were also faced with the challenge of not being able to afford a funeral. In some cases, the family did not claim their deceased and the city buried their loved one, usually in an unmarked grave.

Race/Ethnicity. One's race might complicate the grief process when it was a contributing factor in the death or non-death related losses. Being a Black, Indigenous Person of Color in the United States increases the likelihood of cumulative losses that are related to institutional, societal, historical and ancestral trauma. Additionally, race can be a factor that impacts the grieving process when there are cultural factors that impact help seeking, access to support, and resources in the aftermath of loss.

Resource: Types of Losses Fireside Chat

Did you receive a nugget that helped you? Share with me if you feel moved at thegift@ajitarobinson.com

A reminder: This book does not serve as a replacement for therapy nor is it intended to provide clinical assessment or guidance. Please seek professional guidance and support from a licensed mental health provider in your state of residence for professional support.

FACTORS THAT IMPACT GRIEF

INSTRUCTIONS: There are a variety of factors that can impact the grief process. We have included a few of them here. These factors can be both positive and negative implicatiosn for the bereaved.

The relationship to the deceased

How the news was delivered

Poverty

How the death occurred

The existing support system

Public or private loss

The person's loss history

Nature or Human factor

Religious beliefs/faith tradition

Proximity of death

NOTES:

CHAPTER 4:
Types of Grief

I am often asked: *"How do I know if I'm grieving?" "How do I know if my grief is normal?"* Or *"How do I know if I'm doing this right?"*

Most people navigate grief, in a way that creates a space for healing, renewed purpose and meaning post loss. However, it would be a disservice to not address the complications that one can encounter on the grief journey.

There are a variety of different types of grief that you may notice or experience as you navigate your loss journey. This next section provides a brief overview so that you have information on what to expect. A gentle reminder, your journey is unique. Your body, life experiences, unmet needs, internal dialogue, support systems all play a role in how you manage grief, stress, pain and sorrow.

It is always important to seek professional help when we need it. There are a ton of resources available for those who are navigating the grief journey. Please reach out if you find yourself struggling with navigating the grief journey or even if you just want a safe space to process the loss when your daily life and functioning is completely disrupted, we may need to give ourselves permission to seek a trusted, qualified companion to help us on this journey.

We have already discussed a variety of factors that can impact the grieving process. Some of the factors will be recognizable as contributors to the different types of grief that might emerge.

Disenfranchised grief is when the grief is not recognized by society. We see this often when the bereaved is not recognized or the relationship is not sanctioned. This could occur for a variety of reasons. In the United States, this can be unintentionality reinforced by many corporations that have bereavement policies that only support certain losses. For example, in the African American community fictive kin is a cultural norm. In most corporations, fictive kin would not qualify as a legitimate relative and thus would not qualify for paid time off. This can contribute to disenfranchised grief when the loss isn't recognized by society.

Disenfranchised grief, a term developed by Kenneth Doka, is grief that people experience when they incur a loss that is not, or cannot be openly acknowledged publicly, it is not mourned or socially supported. To disenfranchise one's grief experience requires that an individual, often through societal and/or cultural norms, does not have a right or is not perceived as a person who is grieving.

Individuals who experience disenfranchised grief are not just unacknowledged, forgotten or hidden. Rather, their grief is socially disallowed and unsupported. Kenneth Doka purported that grief could become disenfranchised in three main ways: 1) the loss is not sanctioned. 2) the relationship is not sanctioned or 3) the Grievers themselves are not sanctioned.

DISENFRANCHISED LOSS

Losses that are not sanctioned are disenfranchised when the significance of the loss is not recognized by society. Disenfranchised losses include, but are not limited to loss of body parts, loss of mobility abortion. Disenfranchised losses are often dismissed or minimized. The loss of a beloved pets could fall under this domain.

An example of the loss not being sanctioned include deaths that involve those who die by suicide. Disenfranchised grievers can result when deaths occur in a manner that they are either not well recognized or have significant social stigma.

Disenfranchised grief can also occur in the case of those who are mourning the loss of a loved one who may have died during the commission of a crime or encounter with authority figures such as individuals who died as a result of police brutality. This is particularly compounded by the social, political and historical climate such as the issues surrounding race, privilege and oppression in the United States.

When individuals experience these types of losses, they're often dismissed with statements such as "just get another one", "you are lucky to be alive", or comparative responses that minimizes one's loss experience as it compares to loss experienced by others.

We also have disenfranchised losses that occur when individuals sustain or experience a shift in personality or their way of engaging with the world, which may happen because of psychological changes or biological life outcomes such as dementia.

DISENFRANCHISED GRIEVERS

Disenfranchised grievers are disenfranchised when they are not recognized by society as people who are entitled to experience grief, or who even need to mourn. Oftentimes we overlook that they are grieving, children often fall in this category, as well as the elderly. Individuals who are neurodiverse are often missed as grievers.

Relationships might be disenfranchised when the relationship itself is not granted social approval. These types of relationships might have a secret element that are not publicly acknowledged. For example, relationships between co-workers, friends, teachers, and students. The relationships in these cases might be recognized, in principle, but not as it relates to bereavement. We see this a lot when employers or supervisors, or even therapist are not acknowledged as Grievers for their employees, students, and their clients, respectively.

This also means that if one's grief is disenfranchised; they are less likely to receive the appropriate support and resources needed to navigate their loss. Their grief response might be intensified emotionally and psychologically, it might make it impossible for them to obtain social support and time off from work. These grievers are also likely to be excluded from social mourning rituals such as having the community rally around them, expressing or receiving sympathy and finding solace and inclusion in honoring ceremonies.

Ambiguous Grief is grief that lacks clarity. This can occur is a variety of circumstances such as when the cause of death is unknown or when our soldiers are missing in war and there is no body to bury, or in the case of a kidnapping. This can create difficulty in the grieving process for many.

Complicated (traumatic) grief is also known as traumatic or prolonged grief. The griever may be exhibiting signs that they are globally impacted by the loss. It is often over a long period of time with extreme disruption in functioning such as an inability to maintain relationships, health or employment. This should not be confused with the initial shock that is common in the initial phases of grief. It is not usual for individuals who experience cumulative, racial trauma and ancestral trauma to experience complicated grief.

Anticipatory grief occurs when we begin grieving prior to the loss occurring. In the case of symbolic losses we may experience anticipatory grief when we have separated but haven't finalized the divorce, or when we are preparing for a loved ones transition. Anticipatory grief can occur when we change jobs and we lose our "seniority" or "comfort zone", this can occur even when we are looking forward to the change.

Approximately 7% of people who experience loss, experience acute grief. Acute grief often includes significant somatic distress. An individual experiences acute grief may exhibit a preoccupation with an image of the deceased, guilt that is disproportionate, hostility and alterations in their pre-loss way of conducting themselves. Many individuals who are experiencing acute grief begin to exhibit traits that belong to the deceased, or the individual who has been separated from their life. Individuals who are experiencing acute symptoms of grief may notice a significant delay or distortion in the grief response that leads to an unhealthy, or morbid connection to the deceased.

Acute Grief is a grief process that involves navigate a process that allows the griever to disconnect themselves from the enmeshed connection or bondage to the deceased. The goal of acute grief work is to assist the individual with readjusting and reintegrating to a life that acknowledges the absence of the physical presence of the deceased. Additionally, to assist them in engaging in a process of establishing and maintaining new relationships and connections to the world. We also want to ensure that individuals experiencing acute grief do not engage in avoidant behavior to minimize their grief responses, this delay in the grief process can complicate the grief work.

Lastly, **Frozen grief** is when the bereaved is in a perpetual state of grief. There is no indication that they are moving through the different phases of the grief journey and that there is an unhealthy relationship with the deceased.

This is not an exhaustive list of the different types of losses or types of grief. Rather it is an overview of the common types of grief that we have seen in our work with individuals, families, and children.

Resource on the portal: Grief and Racial Trauma brief discussion

Portal: ajitarobinson.com/giftofgriefresources

NOTES:

CHAPTER 5:

Grief and the Holiday's

The holidays are often a busy time of year that many people look forward to the opportunity to spend with their family and friends. For those who are grieving we might be feeling a bit unanchored. We are sandwiched between a multitude of holidays, anniversaries and other milestone events and are approaching the end of the year and another round of festivities.

We specialize in grief and for many the holiday season can be triggering for a variety of reasons. Grief doesn't take any time off. People often reach out for help navigating the intense feelings of loss and anticipatory angst of navigating yet another round of holiday celebrations and gatherings.

I experienced my own grief spike when celebrating Thanksgiving for the first time after both my grandfather and brother died. The holidays can be bittersweet. While it is a time to spend with family and friends it is also a time when the absence of your loved one is profound. The changes in your relationship status, can make you feel like an outside or a failure.

It also important to acknowledge that we can grieve relationships with people who are physically present. Many of our clients grieve the loss of healthy, supportive relationships with their parents who are still living but unable or unwilling to mend the damage in their relationships. Some may be experiencing grief due to a loss of traditions or because they don't have family to spend this time with.

We work with a lot of students are unable to afford the trip home for the holiday and experience some grief and anxiety around what the holiday might look like for them, and the stress of spending it alone or with a friend's family if they are lucky.

Some of us begin to experience a cascade of emotions ahead of the holiday and may not be aware that anticipatory angst and grief around the holiday season is normal.

The holidays are one time of year that grief can be trigger but anniversaries and other events can be equally triggering. These anniversaries or other special events can catch grievers off guard as they may center around what otherwise is a happy occasion.

We recently worked with a couple in pre-marital counseling where one member of the couple began to engage in avoidant behaviors around wedding planning that created some angst and confusion in the relationship. In our work with this couple we learned that the partner was feeling the impact of both parents being deceased and how to honor the loss and their absence in the wedding ceremony. After discussing the root of the partner behavior, the couple decided to have empty chairs at the ceremony and reception in honor of the deceased.

It is important to note that these life events might trigger the grief response. It is both normal and common for this to happen. Grievers might even begin to anticipate the grief response as these events are approaching and implement a coping strategy or ritual to acknowledge the grief journey.

Here's the other tricky part about the holidays': sometimes being around our family is the trigger. I've worked with hundreds of clients during my career in mental health who have childhood trauma and other wounding that originates in the family of origin. Often these clients feel a responsibility to spend the holiday with family members even when the encounter is sure to wreak havoc on their well-being.

Boundaries are good for self-care. The people who have a problem with your boundaries are usually the ones who benefit from you not having any. It is important that you honor your own need to take care of your mental wellness. This may mean that you limit your interactions with family members who are toxic or otherwise unhealthy. It may mean that you set and maintain firm boundaries regarding your rules of engagement.

It's important that we are mindful of our needs in our grief journey. Here are a few tips to help you navigate grief:

Grief is a full body experience. It is important to remember that grief can be expressed emotionally, physically, psychologically and spiritually. We want to do our best to be present with ourselves and pay attention to what our body is telling us about our needs. **Feel your feelings.** Allow yourself to feel the range of emotions that may show up. Anger, sadness, guilt, and joy are all common and normal reactions to a loss. Give yourself permission to feel your feelings without judging yourself or attempting to inauthentically "change" your feeling.

Be honest that you're grieving. While we may cope differently with grief in a family, it's good to be honest with yourself. Don't struggle to wear a brave face when you're hurting. Express your feelings. Talk to your family and friends. Tell them how you feel. It can help reduce the pain, feelings of loneliness and isolation.

Take breaks. Sometimes being around family and friends can be overwhelming and a reminder of your loss. It's okay to take breaks from interacting and engage in self-care. It's okay to limit your time at holiday functions if being present is too painful.

Create traditions and rituals that honor the loss. Some people find comfort in maintaining traditions and others find meaning in creating new ones. It is important to communicate with your family and loved ones how you all will celebrate the holiday post-loss. The best way to manage this is to plan and support one another.

Do something in memory of the departed loved one. Happy memories can bring a smile to your face. To honor those memories, create something in remembrance of that person. I once knew a young woman who lost her six-year-old son. Her son loved chocolates. She remembered how they used to fight when she refused to buy him the chocolates. When she bought them, he would tell her how he loved her to the moon and back. This memory made her smile. She would buy chocolates and give them to children during Christmas holidays. It made her feel connected to her son.

Find strength from support groups. It's comforting to be around people who wear the same shoes as you. They know where it pinches most. They understand when you say your heart is broken. During the holidays, find a support group in any way you can (religious organizations often offer these kinds of services) and you will get the strength to get through this.

Have an exit strategy. The reality is that grief can be overwhelming and there's no way of knowing how and when it might show up. Sometimes, grief shows up in the midst of joy. If you are planning to attend a function, have a plan for unexpected, overwhelming feelings that may come due to grief. Identify how you can excuse yourself without interfering with others.

Resource on the portal: Deep dive...let's explore the notion of anniversaries, and milestone event and how they impact grief.

Did you receive a nugget that helped you? Share with me if you feel moved at thegift@ajitarobinson.com

NOTES:

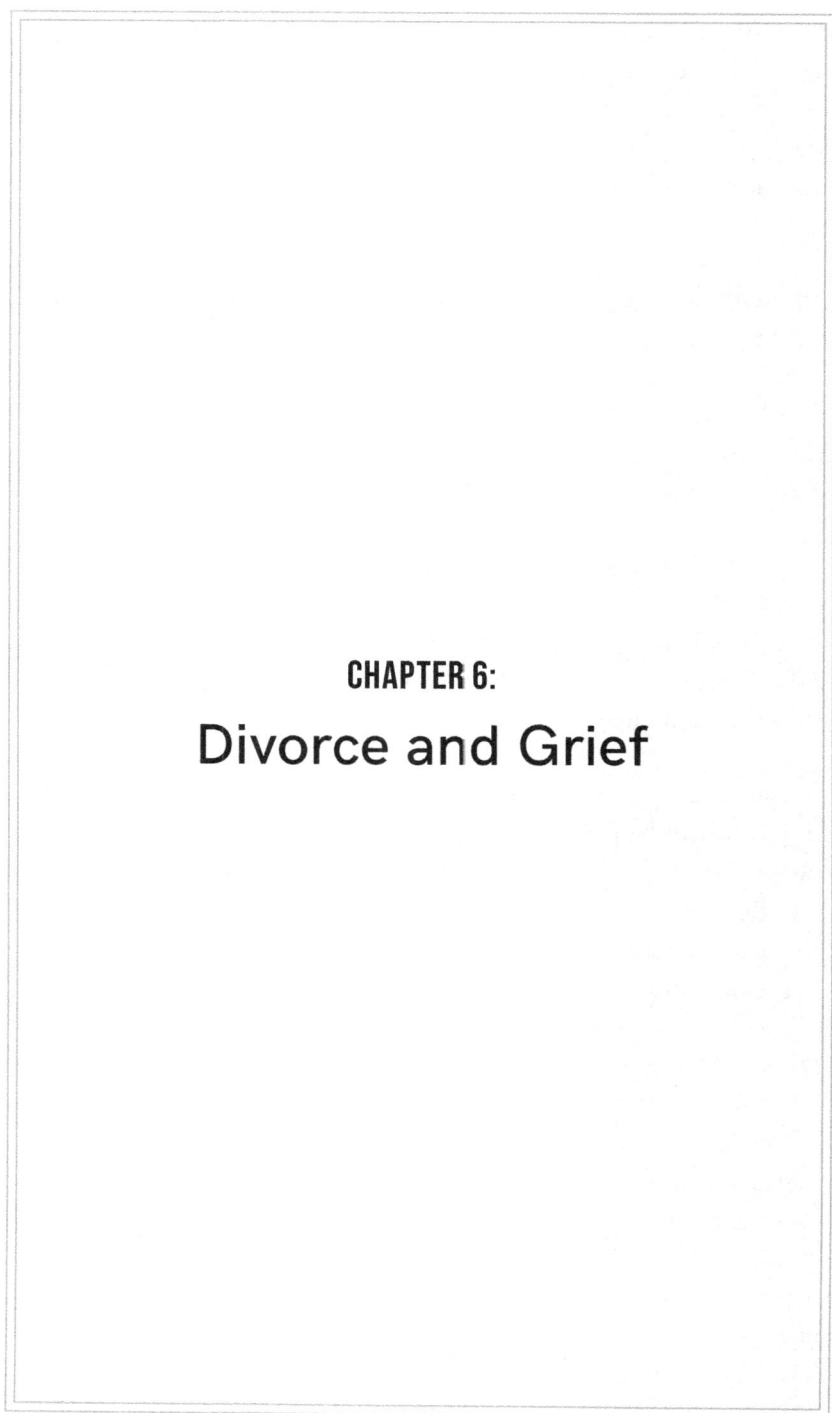

CHAPTER 6:

Divorce and Grief

Divorce is often viewed as a symbolic loss, the loss of a relationship, love, companionship, future plans and so much more. It is important to know that divorce and separation is a loss and it triggers the grief response as well. There are both primary and secondary losses that occur.

The end of a marriage or relationship is a difficult time in your life. You will likely grieve the loss of the kind of future you envisioned, the loss of having a companion to journey life with, the loss of your way of life and so much more. This process can be complicated if children are involved and/or if infertility was a contributor to the dissolution of the relationship. There is a high correlation between infertility and divorce and separation.

The end of a relationship feels like a death for many people. Even if you are the one who initiated the divorce you will still grieve. Each person will navigate the grief process differently and as with any other loss, there is no set length of time. The goal is to create new meaning and engage in life post loss.

While attempting to make sense of life post-separation it is important to be patient with yourself. You will move through your healing process at your own pace. This may involve a range of emotions including anger, denial, sadness, and joy. It is important to seek acceptance that the relationship has ended and that you will make meaning of the experience and you heal from the loss.

During separation and divorce families are faced with a variety of ongoing physical, legal, and emotional tasks. The physical tasks are often demanding and time consuming. The legal tasks are often confusing and expensive. The emotional parts of the separation can take years to resolve.

Separation and divorce are major life transitions involving multiple changes and life decisions which test coping skills and increase levels of stress.

Parents who frequently go back to court and who are experiencing a high degree of conflict with the other parent may have difficulty working through the emotional component.

Parents are called upon to make many important decisions during a time when emotional reserves are low and decision making is exceedingly difficult.

PHYSICAL

Separate/move out

Mom's Home/Dad's Home

Moving out of area

Living with other relatives

Transporting kids to school and other places

LEGAL

Consider legal options

File and serve legal papers

Decide financial issues

Decide custody issues

Make a parenting plan

Finalize the divorce

EMOTIONAL

Move through the grief process

Manage conflict

Develop coping and problem-solving skills

Work on co-parenting relationships

Work on parent-child relationships

Learn single parenting skills

Ask for help and support

Establish new relationships

WHEN ANGER SHOWS UP...

Anger often gets a bad rap when it comes to self-expression and mourning. Anger is a natural and sometimes protective part of the grief process. It is important that we give ourselves permission to peel back the layers of our feelings...anger often is the emotion that is most readily accessible, but it is often a mask for sadness, fear, distrust, etc.

Anger often shows up in the grief process especially for individuals navigating divorce or separation. It is important to keep the following in mind:

1. **Recognize when you are angry and be aware of the many faces of anger including** irritability, feeling upset, negative mood, brooding, negative attitude, defiance, arguing, frustration etc. Rate your anger on a scale of 1-10. At what point on the scale might you want to remove yourself from the situation and take a break, so that you don't say or do something you might regret?

2. **Once you recognize that you are angry, stop, think, and make a choice.** Knowing that you are angry, do you want to allow the anger to escalate, or back off and separate? Backing off and separating is the wise choice in most interactions when anger is perpetuating an argument, defensiveness, or resistance. Anger that intimidates is abusive. Once you back off, you may need at least 20 minutes alone to calm down. You may want to warn others if you are in an angry mood.

3. **Be aware that anger can cover up other emotions, such as hurt, and feeling abandoned.** Expressing anger inappropriately won't relieve the underlying hurt that you feel. If the person fights back, the hurt can become deeper and broader in scope.

4. **Be aware that anger can be a trigger.** Don't let your anger control your decisions or prompt behavior that is destructive in a relationship. Many people look for someone to attack when they are angry. This rarely creates resolution to the anger. Allowing your anger to explode is never a good idea.

5. **Work through your anger about the past.** Grieving a relationship means letting go of anger. How angry you are at your ex-mate indicates the level of strong feelings you still feel towards him/her. Work on getting over it and letting go. Holding a grudge will not help to resolve anger. Decide to let go of grudges, which represent anger from the past.

6. **Never use your child as a weapon against your ex-mate or a dumping ground for your anger.** Anger is easily turned into hostility, resentment and revenge. Intense anger is frightening, confusing, and damaging to children. Complaining about the ex-spouse to the child puts that child in the middle, which is unfair and emotionally damaging.

7. **Find appropriate outlets for your anger.** Talk to friends. Join a support group. Get counseling to help work through the anger so that it does not consume you. Learn to express concerns without getting angry and without verbally attacking the person with whom you are angry. Walk it off. Take deep breaths. Take 20-30 minute breaks when worked up. Keep heated conversations short.

8. **If you continue to be angry and cannot stop there, seek professional assistance.** There are many types of therapists and anger management courses to help you manage anger. Chronic anger may also indicate an underlying depression. Getting assessed for depression by a therapist or psychiatrist may help to determine the next course of action to reduce anger and improve your overall happiness.

There are similarities between grieving losses due to the death of a loved one and grieving losses due to separation and divorce such as:

- A deep sense of abandonment

- A deep sense of loss

There are also differences such as:

- Cultural and societal rituals for death, but none for separation and divorce

All family members must grieve the multiple losses associated with separation and divorce. During this time, coping skills are tested, and people can become overwhelmed.

- If the separation is unexpected and comes without warning people are often not prepared to deal with it.

- Sometimes grief can include obsession, when you cannot stop thinking about the loss or situation.

- Sometimes people get caught in a specific emotional state such as anger, hostility, sadness or depression.

SELF-CARE TIPS POST-DIVORCE AND SEPARATION

- **Make time each day to nurture yourself.** Help yourself heal by scheduling daily time for activities you find calming and soothing. Go for a walk-in nature, listen to music, enjoy a hot bath, get a massage, read a favorite book, take a yoga class, or savor a warm cup of tea.

- **Pay attention to what you need** in any given moment and speak up to express your needs. Honor what you believe to be right and best for you even though it may be different from what your ex or others want. Say "no" without guilt or angst as a way of honoring what is right for you.

- **Stick to a routine.** A divorce or relationship breakup can disrupt almost every area of your life, amplifying feelings of stress, uncertainty, and chaos. Getting back to a regular routine can provide a comforting sense of structure and normalcy.

- **Take a time out.** Try not to make any major decisions in the first few months after a separation or divorce, like starting a new job or moving to a new city. If you can, wait until you're feeling less emotional so that you can make better decisions.

- **Avoid using alcohol, drugs, or food to cope.** When you're in the middle of a breakup, you may be tempted to do anything to relieve your feelings of pain and loneliness. But using alcohol, drugs, or food as an escape is unhealthy and destructive in the long run. It is essential to find healthier ways of coping with painful feelings

- **Explore new interests.** A divorce or breakup is a beginning as well as an end. Take the opportunity to explore new interests and activities. Pursuing fun, new activities gives you a chance to enjoy life in the here-and-now, rather than dwelling on the past.

DIVORCE, GRIEF AND KIDS

Divorce is a life altering moment not only for parents but for the children of this union, what we are discussing applies to adult children, and separation that doesn't involve divorce. Many children will recall this experience for a lifetime. Facing children to tell them about divorce can be the most difficult aspect of the divorce process. Parents often have anxiety about delivering the news that emerges from guilt and shame. There are often concerns for the child's ability to understand what is happening and a desire to shield them from any possible pain. The process should involve intentional timing by the parents, a neutral statement explaining what is happening, and a brief overview of what is going to happen to the family in the future. It is important that parents work together to share the news of divorce to the children. More harm can be done if a parent breaks the news without their co-parent or shares the information in a way that is toxic or attempts to manipulate the children into taking sides. It is vital that children are given reassurances to help through the adjustment period.

Note: We are intentionally using "parent" to honor the diverse family structures that exist. An overarching assumption is that abuse and/or neglect are not contributing factors.

PREPARING FOR THE ANNOUNCEMENT

- In the weeks leading up to the actual separation, parents should take the opportunity to discuss the separation and divorce process. Do not tell children until you are certain of the decision

- Consider the child's routine and how different aspects of that routine may change. Try to focus on the gains instead of losses. For example, explaining dad will make dinner when they come to the parents' new home instead of one parent making dinner for the family.

- Present a united front when telling your children about divorce. Reassure the parental roles to avoid possible future feelings of resentment and anger from both parent and child.

- Work together to practice a script for the conversation that is clear and simple. Avoid any blame statements that may prevent the child from maintaining a positive relationship with each parent.

- Set aside time for the discussion and try to answer their questions. Prepare yourself to be honest, in an appropriate way, while keeping anger and hurt in check.

- Remember, the discussion is to explain an adult decision and you are there to deal with the child's feelings, fears, and needs.

Plan how you will break the news

If possible, involve both parents in this. Reassure your kids that both of you will still be their parents, even if you will not all be together.

Remember, younger kids do not need much detail but be honest with them. Older kids might need a little more explanation. The explanation should always be done in an age-appropriate way.

For example, it would be inappropriate to state that the parents are divorcing because (parent) had an affair with a colleague. Children rarely benefit from these details. They aren't often shared for the benefit of the children, but rather from a space of wounding experienced by one of the adults. It might be more useful to explain that the parents have tried to fix the issues between them but sometimes things can't be fixed once they are broken.

Keep it clear to your kids that you love them as always.

Both of you need to assure your kids that you are going to take care of them. Tell them that you will often meet as a family and be together.

Let your kids know that they are not the cause of divorce

Some children might silently suffer and worry that they are the cause of your separation. Let them know that nothing they did caused the divorce. Help them understand that they can't change anything.

Encourage your kids to express their feelings

Speaking out is an effective strategy for releasing tension. Your kids might be reluctant to open up, but you should encourage them to do so.

Let them say what they feel. It is by speaking out that children heal and learn to adjust.

If they can't talk to you, find a mental health professional or any other person they can talk to freely.

Help them to mourn.

The divorce of parents is like the death of a loved one to a child. It pains and hurts because they feel life is going to be different without one parent, and the life that they are familiar.

Tell them about the changes they should expect

Talk to your children about how you are going to live after the divorce. Who is going to live with them? How often will you be getting together as a family? What visitation arrangements have you made?

Let them know that they can still relate to the extended family

Some children might think that separating from one parent means separation with the respective family of the other partner. Keep it clear that they can still have a close relationship with the extended family.

Let them know that they can love the other parent.

While there may be resentful feelings between you and your partner, your children are not part of it. Don't talk negatively about the other parent. Let the kids know that they have the best parents despite the fact that you are no longer a good fit for one another.

WHAT SHOULDN'T YOU TELL YOUR KIDS?

Even though some children are old enough to ask why you divorced, avoid telling them anything that will cause them to hate the other parent. These include:

Things that made you dislike the other parent

Reaching the point of divorce means that you had enough of whatever dynamics were present in the relationships. Even if you had a list of bad reasons, do not tell your children. It might turn them against the parent, and this is unfair to your child.

What you feel about your former partner's choices

Your ex might make some decisions after a divorce that you find questionable. Don't let your kids know how you feel about it because it may affect their relationships. Instead, talk to a counselor or a close friend about it.

Divorce can take an emotional toll on the ones going through it, but it also hard on the children. It may take some time for them to adjust.

However, if you notice specific reactions from your kids after a divorce, do not ignore them. They can be serious red flags. If your kids experience depression, anxiety, a change in sleeping and eating habits, or aggressive behavior, you should call a therapist or your primary care provider for a referral.

As parents, kids desire that both of you be involved in their lives. Appreciate them. Show interest in everything they do.

Make regular calls and stay connected. Talk directly with the other parent when coordinating care and other adult decision related to the kids. Work together for the sake of your children's happiness.

Check out the chart below and review some of the changes you might notice in your child in response to divorce, separation, and grief.

Resource on the portal: Hop on over to the portal and grab the script to help you have this conversation with your child.

Did you receive a nugget that helped you? Share with me if you feel moved at thegift@ajitarobinson.com

AGE LEVEL REACTIONS OF CHILDREN TO SEPARATION AND DIVORCE

Age plays a role in how kids react to separation and divorce.

No matter what age your children are, never fight or argue with the other parent in front of them!

Pre-School (1-4)	**Behaviors:**	Bedwetting, clinging, crying, whining, tantrums, aggression, biting, hitting, yelling
	Thoughts/ Feelings:	Intense occasional sadness/crying, anger, and low frustration tolerance. Fear of abandonment, needing to be close, separation anxiety.
	What parents can do:	Reassure them of being loved. Provide consistency, warmth and understanding. Set firm limits on misbehaviors with appropriate consequences (i.e. brief time outs of 3-5 minutes)
5-7 Year Olds	**Behaviors:**	Tantrums, crying, bed-wetting, attempts to get parents back together.
	Thoughts/ Feelings:	Worry, "I'm to blame," temper tantrums.
	What parents can do:	Set clear limits and consequences. Offer age appropriate explanations. Allow consistent contact with both parents. Keep consistent schedules and routines. Reassure them of being loved.

8-12 Year Olds	**Behaviors:**	Rejection of one parent, apathy, acting out, fighting, defiance/being oppositional, somatic complaints or perfectionism.
	Thoughts/ Feelings:	Shame, blame, insecure, sadness, "Whose fault is the divorce?", powerless, denial, "It's no big deal."
	What parents can do:	Encourage kids to talk and share feelings and thoughts, teach anger management, validate grief. Be flexible in permitting kids to talk to and see the other parent.
13-18 Year Olds	**Behaviors:**	Increased risk for drug/alcohol use, promiscuity, defiance, argumentativeness, controlling behaviors, may reject one or both parents, increased risk for incorrigibility, withdrawal.
	Thoughts/ Feelings:	Sad, confused, angry, resentful, apathy.
	What parents can do:	Be flexible in visitation schedule, collaborate with adolescents in addressing their needs and wants.
Adult Children of Divorce	**Behaviors:**	Fear of commitment, distrust of opposite sex, fear of success, apprehensions about marriage.
	Thoughts/ Feelings:	Unresolved identity issues, mild depression.
	What parents can do:	Do not use adult children as confidants. Don't put down the other parent. Validate their struggles. Monitor functioning. Both parents need to stay closely connected with adult children. Provide a warm environment for young adults to visit that is a home.

NOTES:

CHAPTER 7:

Children and Grief

"Time is an unopened gift for many. Be fully present, today."
– Dr. Ajita Robinson

Children's grief is particularly unique in that they may not be developmentally able to express their grief through words. Sometimes, if we are not careful, we may even overlook the ways in which children grieve.

In 2014 my family suffered the loss of my great grandmother, my daughter's great great grandmother. I am thankful that they had a chance to meet. This was the first loss of a person that my daughter remembers firsthand. She remembers losing our family cat, in 2016, to breast cancer. I vividly remember the sadness of having to tell my daughter that Grandma Pearline had died. I remember feeling unprepared. I, a counselor who talks to other people's children all day about death and dying, was terrified to talk to my own. It had hit home.

I felt empty and scared. I was also angry. Someone, well intentioned, decided to tell my child that grandma Pearline died in her sleep. I remember anticipating the questions, the fear of going to bed. And they did come. Two months later. She stopped sleeping through the night. She no longer enjoyed the freedom of having her own room. There was just fear.

My training was failing me when faced with the pain I witnessed in my child's face as well as the loss I was feeling. Numerous conversations and prayer reminded me that Grief is a Gift and that I could choose to show my daughter the beauty of honoring our loved ones in our daily lives. This felt more manageable. Perhaps, because I was back in my zone of being able to use my knowledge and skills as a counselor to balance the deep grief I was experiencing. We turned to story-telling as our way of honoring Grandma Pearline. Grief is universal, yet a unique experience for each of us. While I wanted to model that grieving was okay, I also wanted to respect that my daughter's way would be different than my own.

As a society, we spend some much of our time and energy trying to beat death, when in fact it is one of the absolutes that we can count on. We will all die, eventually. Yet, it's this absolute truth that we avoid discussing, many times, until it's too late. The reality is, children grieve, and they grieve quite differently than adults.

What kids need to know? The simple answer is: the truth. This is probably the statement that scares parents and caregivers the most. So, let's make it a little less scary because grief is hard enough.

Kids need to know that they are safe. Death often calls into question our own mortality. Kids will often wonder if Mom and Dad are going to die. We should answer these questions, truthfully, but in an age appropriate way. According to research on cognitive development, we understand that children ages 5-7 still believe in magical thinking, thus death is not viewed as permanent. In comparison, a teenager may have lost a classmate to neighborhood violence or a school shooting and is aware that death is permanent.

DO CHILDREN GRIEVE?

The short answer is yes. It is important to understand that the way children grieve is impacted by their developmental stage and their individual cognitive capacity can play an important role in determining how a child or adolescent deals with loss, how their bereavement experience may manifest and its impact on subsequent development (see chart on pages 79-80).

WHAT IMPACTS HOW CHILDREN GRIEVE?

When discussing children and adolescent grief it is critical that we consider that one's understanding of the concept of death changes over time and is often relevant to developmental stage. As we look at grief in children and adolescence, we must acknowledge that childhood grief is not merely a different version of adult mourning, but rather one that is unique to children. There are some unique markers that occur during the sub-stages of development, as compared to later timeframes in development.

For example, it is more common in younger children to experience regressive behaviors such as bedwetting or thumb sucking, separation anxiety abandonment, fear of others, dying, fear of their own mortality, or feeling responsible for the event. Young children often engage in magical thinking and they may not understand that it is permanent and irreversible. Young children may struggle to understand that death is universal. Children at this stage of development often struggle with understanding that individuals who have died, are not functional and thus do not require life sustaining tasks such as eating and sleeping.

However, grief in later childhood is more likely to manifest as learning difficulties, changes in behavior, difficulty with socialization and anger, to name a few. Factors that can impact the grief process of children and adolescence are the level of available support (familial, social, peer), method of notification and cognitive maturation of the child.

Adolescent grief is a multifaceted process, as it is in other life stages.

There are a variety of reactions that are normal that include:

Feeling different from one's peer group. This is an important aspect to pay attention to because adolescence is a time in which adolescents most identify with their peer group and often take great effort to fit in. Feeling different from one's peers can lead to suffering and distress for adolescents.

Other ways that grief might manifest in adolescence are an observed decrease in social competency, changes in mood, feeling guilty, anger, intense feelings of powerlessness and hopelessness.

Acting out and attention seeking behaviors. For many adolescents these behaviors are generally designed to seek help and should not be conflated to assume self-injury is the goal.

Inability to concentrate, focus unfinished tasks, which can result in academic challenges and missed milestones.

Unlike younger children, adolescents are aware and understand that death is a natural part of life for many, assuming that the cognitive capacity and developmental trajectory aligns with chronological age, adolescents, often understand that death means a future without that person (or non-death related change). However, it is very jarring for adolescents when a peer or friend dies. Oftentimes the death of other adolescents is sudden or violent, which is the case in suicides, homicides, and other accidental deaths.

We may see questioning in adolescents that are more philosophical in nature. They might question why these unimaginable, painful, and often preventable events have occurred. Grief, particularly death, can raise issues of one's own personal mortality, possibly for the first time. It is important to be mindful that the loss of a parent or loss in adolescence is often positively correlated with increased engagement in risky behaviors such as drinking, driving, and sexual promiscuity.

TALKING TO KIDS ABOUT DEATH AND DYING

When talking to kids about death and dying we want to remember that children's capacity to understand death changes over time as their cognitive and developmental capacities change.

When discussing death, dying and grief with children we want to take the individual child's needs into consideration so that we can use chronological and developmentally appropriate language to describe the events (death and non-death related losses). For example, young children often need to be told on numerous occasions that death is final and irreversible. They might engage in behaviors where they look for the deceased because young children do not understand the permanence of death. It is important that guardians, healers, and helpers who are working with children understand and explain, often more than once, that a loved one is not returning. Children often think in concrete terms, so we need to use language that matches their way of thinking and processing style.

We want to avoid terms such as "Daddy is sleeping" to describe death. Parents and guardians often use these terms to protect children from being sad or hurt. However, it can have the reserve effect if children become afraid of going to sleep because "Daddy went to sleep and never awakened."

Instead, we might state: "Daddy's heart stopped working. Daddy died."

We want to give concrete explanations that are age appropriate so that children not only understand the loss, but they also understand that they did not cause the other person's death or the non-death related event. Young children are quite egocentric, in such they often believe they have more power than they do in these situations. This is also the case when parents' divorce or separate, children might believe that they are to blame.

One's ability to cope with loss changes, as one matures. Children might try to seek comfort from others. Children might seemingly deny (cognitively and verbally) the impact of the loss. They may not have words to express their feelings. We often see the impact of grief on children through their play, delays or disruptions in development milestones, and behavioral coping strategies (both adaptive and maladaptive).

The research is clear and consistent, that support from caregivers, parental support and encouragement, are key factors with respect to bereavement outcomes for children and adolescence.

Children who were identified as resilient after experiencing the loss of a parent, or the loss of a primary caregiver reported receiving more warmth and more discipline, more structure, compared to their peers who experienced a variety of mental health challenges following the death.

In children who exhibited more significant mental health challenges, there were more significant loss of structure, and loss of availability of positive support.

Parents and caregiver's ability to learn how to recognize grief in children and adolescents is necessary to help them develop effective coping strategies and can help create positive transitional outcomes for grieving children.

Facing the reality of the loss of a loved one, or the loss of relationship or the change in the family system may ultimately strengthen existing coping strategies. Having positive coping mechanisms in the face of subsequent stressful life events may also result in decreased negative emotional or physical consequences or lead to positive outcomes. It is important to remember that this is an individual experience. However, taking psychosocial, emotional, physical and cognitive capacity of the child and adolescent into consideration as we develop appropriate coping skills and support to help children adolescent can help children acquire tools and language to create meaning in their own way in life post loss.

Why it's important to talk to kids about death and dying?

It's a universal fact of life. It's important that you understand what they "know" so that you can correct any misinformation… misinformation can lead to fears that can a lasting effect on children's narrative around loss and how they navigate future losses. Talking about it helps us understand what their needs are so we can adequately support them.

What to say?

I am often asked, "What should I say to my child?" "How do I explain the death (or loss) to my child in a way that they can understand it?"

The answer is complicated. It depends.

It depends on their age and their life experiences. It depends on your beliefs about what happens when we die. This is a unique conversation that should honor your child's right to know the truth and that is anchored in your beliefs. Remember, children are incredibly resilient when they have consistent, supportive adults in their life.

Our stuff will often dictate what we believe is important to tell children. Our stuff includes our beliefs, our own experiences with loss and grief, and our relationship to the loss. Also, when we are prompted to have the discussion might influence what one says. Do we feel READY? Or are we forced to have the conversation due to 1) an event/loss/crisis? Or 2) exposure via media/school/etc.

What kids need to know?

They are loved.

They are not alone.

They are important.

It is not their fault.

They are safe.

When talking to and helping grieving children we also want to honor that despite their age, children are autonomous beings. We often want to protect and buffer children from normal life occurs but sometimes, specifically related to grief, its impossible. Attempting to disrupt or prevent children from grieving can cause greater harm.

Be simple in your communication. Be straightforward rather than trying to come up with euphemisms that often distract from the child's experience. "I'm sorry your Dad died" is more effective than fluff.

Respect their feelings. Allow children to grief in their own way. You will not make children feel better by attempting to distract them from their grief. It generally makes them feel unheard and unseen.

Be patient. Children often repeat questions and the story of their loss. They need to do this to make meaning of the experience and to begin to grabble with the reality of the loss. They aren't intended to shock you or be dismissive of your feelings. They are managing grief in bits of pieces because that is developmentally how their bodies deal with pain.

Be consistent. Do what you say you are going to do. Visit them if you say you will. Return when you say you will and communicate when there is a change in plans. Consistency = safety for children.

Grief can impact academics. Grief can affect the child's ability to attend to new material, may result in decreased motivation, concentration and more. See table in Chapter on Children and Divorce.

Children benefit from formal supports. Do not be afraid to seek professional support for your child. Sometimes children need to know that they are not the only one experiencing a loss. Finding a group or therapist that can help the child process their loss can be very helpful on their journey.

Resource in the portal: Hop on a download our Grief Kit for Kids

Did you receive a nugget that helped you? Share with me if you feel moved at thegift@ajitarobinson.com

NOTES:

CHAPTER 8:

Social Media and Grief

Social media at its core function is a group of websites and applications that, allow users to create, share content and participate in social networking. For many social media is utilized to access community, information, and to socialize in a way that may not be possible in their local society. People might use social media as a way of connecting with people across the world, as well as to share content that educates, entertains, and inspires.

However, we have all heard of some of the cons, and the limitations of social media, that might impact one's privacy. There is some indication that it may have some implications for one's mental health. Social media can be utilized as a coping mechanism can take up, lots of time and one can lose control of how their information is shared. Parents may feel a loss of control over what information their children might be exposed to. Even though individual profiles may be private they are still interacting on an open public forum. It is also an easy way to get content useful content in front of a wider audience.

Approximately 15% of consumers use social networking sites to search for local businesses, roughly 71% of users say that they're more likely to purchase from a brand, they follow online. Social networks and blogs now also account for a quarter of the total time, Americans spend on online.

Roughly 73% of adults indicate that they utilize a social networking site of some kind, and 42% of online adults use multiple social networking sites and have an average of two to three online profiles, 63% indicate that they visit Facebook daily, 57% visit Instagram daily, and 40% of cell phone owners use a social networking site on their phone.

Social media is an accessible tool used to connect people with brands, information, and the world.

On average, 135 minutes are spent on social media everyday by global Internet users. We also know that teens and young adults are likely to utilize social media two to three times this amount with millennials being the largest group of social media users at 90% Gen Xers at 77.5% and baby boomers at 48.2%.

So, as you can see, individuals utilize social media on a regular basis for casual engagement, entertainment, and information. Given the frequency and consistency in use it makes sense that when even when one is grieving this behavior might continue. During grief, it's important that we are mindful of the ways that our social media usage might positively and negatively impact our grief process, and our mental health and wellness overall.

In this next section we are going to talk about the intersection of social media and mental health and then a discussion of social media and grief, and factors that might impact the grieving process in both promotive and inhibiting ways. The impact that social media can have on health and wellness, specifically mental health and the grief process is not on a continuum, it is a constantly changing process that is unique to the individual and the situation. We don't want to pathologize or create any stigma around the utilization of social media, we want to take a balanced approach. This also means that those of you who are supporting individuals who have experienced a loss, understand that their social media behavior might change, and they may have different needs with respect to social media. We will discuss the etiquette regarding social media and grief for grievers and their companions.

SOCIAL MEDIA AND MENTAL HEALTH

Emotions expressed online can impact your mood whether these are emotions that you are directly expressing or these same emotions you are being exposed to, and can even provoke instances of feeling, joy, happiness depression or sadness. The range of emotions one feels can be influenced by your own mental health status, as well as what you are exposed to. There is some evidence that suggests that increased use of social media platforms can create emotionally contagious experiences that can affect your mental health in both positive and negative ways. Most of the research that has been conducted regarding social media downplays the positive impact that social media can have. Many of these studies are legitimate.

However, there is evidence to suggest that addiction to social media is an epidemic among our nation's teens and young adults, but this also does not seem to be limited to the United States. One of the downsides of social media is that nearly half of the sources of information that one can be exposed to can create negative effect within the users. This is particularly true for those who might be already struggling with negative internal dialogue, and decreased self-esteem. Instagram, known for its beautiful curated feeds can leave one feeling less than, unable to keep up, disconnected, and different from their peers. We have also seen a vicious cycle of cyberbullying occur on social media.

However, there are tons of studies that also suggest that social media can have positive benefits. We want to provide a balanced view of social media so that one might weigh the pros and cons and allow everyone to make more informed decisions as it relates to our mental health and wellness. Social media platforms can help with feeling engaged and connected. Many users who connect with others on social media, particularly those who belong to curated groups such as crafting, arts, music travel and other interest related groups report feeling an alleviation of feelings of social isolation and loneliness and an increased connection with individuals who share similar beliefs and values. Social media also allows users, a certain level of anonymity to express their mental illness challenges, to express their feelings without danger of stigma or safety concerns. It also creates access to useful information from peers, and trusted sources. It might also inspire healthy lifestyle changes. Social media can be utilized as a motivational tool to achieve a healthy lifestyle such as losing weight engaging in self-care, creating a bedtime routine, going to the gym, cooking fresh foods, starting a garden, and so on. Oftentimes, it can also create a sense of accountability and connectedness with others, and we can leverage this to create a community that positively reinforces the changes that we want to make in our life.

Social media as an accountability tool is most common when we announce a goal that we have for ourselves on social media, and our social support system rallies around us to share positive affirmations, to check in, and to be sources of support. Having the ability to share this experience with others might create an accountability group, or sense of connectedness.

Social media was also helpful and responsible for being able to safely connect users with networks and interventions to keep them safe. For example, Facebook, has integrated and connected with the 24-hour suicide prevention hotlines as a source of intervention for individuals who might be experiencing suicidal thoughts and ideations. The social site provides an anonymous option to help connect people to resources and support. It also allows for individuals to sign up for services where they might receive daily advice, motivational messages, and other information that's useful to promote recovery, wellness and restoration.

Social media sites such as a meet ups creates a sense of community for individuals who are local, who have shared interest, who belong to clubs, and organizations. Twitter has a feature called tweet ups which are face to face meetups that are organized online involving people with similar interests. These are all things that help promote connection between individuals who share the same interest or are exploring new interests and help create new relationships.

GRIEF AND SOCIAL MEDIA

I remember the day as clear as yesterday. At the time that I am writing this chapter, it's officially the 2-year anniversary of my brothers' death. I will never forget the phone call I received from my father telling me that my brother was being rushed to the Emergency room and that he was not conscious. He was found at the bottom of a swimming pool. There were so many details that were missing, so many questions swirling around in my head. A major part of the grief process is trying to understand what has occurred, how we got to this place. Many of us embark on a fact-finding mission to learn as much as we can about our loved one's final moments. What happened? How did this happen? Who else was there? Was he in pain?

An unimaginable thing happened during this process. I have a large family and it took a while to notify all our family members. For some reason, we were having an issue getting a hold of my other brother. The one thing I tried to prevent happened. My surviving brother learned about of brothers' death via Facebook. In addition to feeling helpless I was now livid that people would be so insensitive in spreading the news article and tagging my brother (deceased) without taking into consideration that the family had not been notified.

Social media is not all bad when it comes to the grief journey as mentioned above. However, it can present unique challenges for the bereaved. In addition to friends sharing the news articles and asking questions we also encountered numerous requests from the media due to the public nature of his death.

A few things we want to keep in mind regarding our own grief journey and social media is that our need for privacy and the way we utilize social media is unique to each of us.

Some people might use social media to memorialize and honor their loved one. They might enjoy seeing the love and tributes shared about their loved one and for others it might be an overwhelming experience. I found that I experienced a range of emotions: happiness at how well loved he was and resentment towards people saying things that were well intentioned but insensitive, nonetheless.

The following is not a list of do's and don'ts but rather a list of things to consider. For those of you who might be navigating a loss, but also for those of you who are companions to others who are grieving.

You might consider:

Following the families lead on communicating about the loss and specific events

Offering your condolences

Not bombarding the family with phone calls, DMs, tags, and texts

Being patient with loved ones who are navigating the loss of a loved one

Send food or flowers to the family

Respecting the family's privacy

Participate in memorial or honoring rituals as they are shared by the family

You might consider refraining from:

Reading the comments (on news articles and other threads)

Asking what happened (this is often insensitive and inappropriate if the family has not outright disclosed this information)

Saying "they're in a better place" this is often well intentioned but may not be helpful to the family who would much rather their loved one be with them

Break the "news" before the family has shared the information

Tag family in your posts. Their notifications are likely overwhelming.

Center yourself. This is especially important if you had a conflicted or undisclosed relationship with the deceased, it is likely to cause more harm in the immediate aftermath of a loss.

Saying "time will heal" this is a well-intentioned statement but is not accurate for grief work.

Get/Have another. This is often said to people who have miscarried or lost a pet. This is inappropriate and insensitive and minimizes the loss.

For bereaved individuals' social media can be a part of the healing and honoring process and can negatively impact the grievers experience. For some, social media is a safe place to distract themselves from the reality of their loss and for others it serves as a constant reminder of that which is no more.

These responses and tips are relevant for physical and symbolic losses.

Resource in the portal: Family Statements and a 5-minute video exploring grief and social media

Did you receive a nugget that helped you? Share with me if you feel moved at thegift@ajitarobinson.com

NOTES:

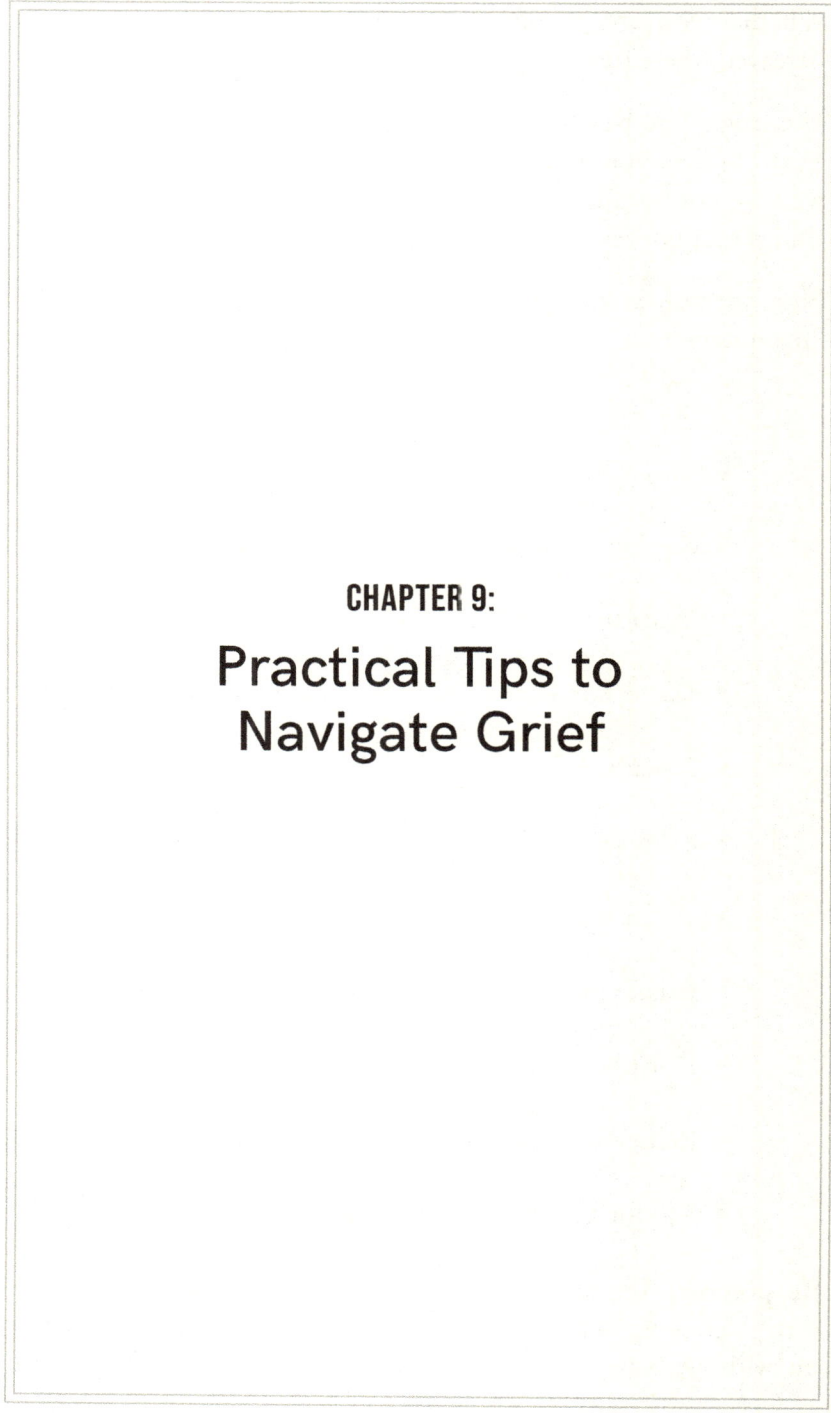

CHAPTER 9:

Practical Tips to Navigate Grief

Whether you are grieving or serving as a companion for the bereaved, these tips are useful for you regardless of your role.

This might also be a helpful reference for those who might ask how they can help you during your grief journey. In the midst of grief, we may not be able to ask for help, so this list serves as a guide of things that grievers often find helpful on this journey.

Here are basic guidelines for the grief process regardless of the loss encountered:

- Allow yourself time to grieve.

- Anticipate unexpected changes.

- Get lots of support from friends and other parents.

- Don't try to be a superhero.

- Take good care of your physical and emotional health.

- Beware of the rebound.

- Keep a journal.

- Try to stick to a normal schedule.

- Expect to be reminded of the past occasionally.

- Don't be hard on yourself or overly self-critical.

- Remember that it takes time to adjust to multiple changes.

- Ask for help when you need it.

Be present. The amount of time you spend with a loved one who is grieving is less important than the quality of time. Show up without being rushed, be fully present. Listen without judgment, offer compassionate companionship. Normalize everything. Be okay with silence. Take care of yourself so that you have the resources to hold space for the griever.

Be respectful. Do not talk down to the bereaved or engage in disrespectful behavior or language if you are the griever. Grievers might engage in childlike behavior out of their grief, be respectful in your correction or care-frontation (if its necessary). If another person is in the room discussing the griever, make sure you include them in the conversation and speak directly to them rather than talk about them as if they are not present. This happens often with children and vulnerable adults.

Avoid judgment. Try to keep "should have", "could have" and "would have" out of the conversation. Be mindful of your facial expressions and what messages your non-verbal communication might be sending to the griever.

Don't go everything by yourself. It is so hard to be on the receiving end of help. Don't become a one-person show whether you are grieving or serving as a companion. Allow family, friends, clergy and neighbors to be apart of your support circle. Don't try to fix everything- some issues may not require fixing while others can be put on hold.

Grieve and live. Very few bereaved people grieve continuously. We often grieve in cycles, and may re-grieve as a result of triggers (e.g. anniversaries, holidays, and milestones). It is okay to live in the present moment, experience joy and adventure and still grieve. Sometimes we need permission to take a break from grief- to think about or do something else.

Rest and hydrate. Self-care is so important on this journey. It is common that people develop flu and colds and other illnesses during grief and compassion fatigue when serving as companions. You cannot serve from an empty cup and grief work takes a lot of your body's energy.

Rituals related to death, dying and the deceased include, but not limited to:

- Funerals, memorial services, shiva are common mourning rituals

- Nine nights of mourning celebration is a custom common in many Caribbean cultures

- Offering or preparation of food to be shared with family and others who are grieving. This may occur days before or after the funeral.

- In some communities it is customary to host a gathering after the funeral services. In some communities' family and friends provide food and refreshment in others the family of the deceased hosts and provides food.

- Signing the guest book at a funeral service

- Sending a card of condolences and sharing memories of the deceased

- Sending mass cards to catholic church or funeral home

- Sending flowers

- Sending a donation to a charity chosen by the family or in honor of the deceased

- In some Jewish communities having the funeral as quickly as possible shows a sign of respect to the deceased. Following the funeral, Jewish members may observe Shiva, or seven days of mourning after the funeral is held at the home of the mourner.

- Bringing gifts of fruit to the mourners

- Preparation of the body may occur at home in preparation for cremation is common in many Hindu traditions

- In some Muslim tradition's mourners may offer words of condolences and help the bereaved come to understand and accept God's will. The mourning period might be 3 days except for the spouse who may mourn for 4 months and 10 days.

Rituals that may be helpful in times of mourning physical or symbolic losses:

- Lighting a candle at certain, special times of the day or week to remind you or your loved one (for example, at dinnertime to represent sharing meals with him or her)

- Creating a memory scrapbook and filling it with photographs, letters, postcard, notes or other significant memorabilia from your life together. This can also be done as a way of creating or imaging life post separation, job loss, or as a vision board for the future.

- Spending time listening to your loved one's favorite music or creating a special mix of music that reminds you of that person.

- Watching their favorite movie

- Planting a tree or flowers in your loved one's memory

- Visiting your loved one's burial site

- Carrying something special that reminds you of your loved one that you can take out and hold or touch when you feel the need; necklaces and bracelets are common

- Creating a work of art in your loved one's memory

- Preparing and eating a special meal in honor of your loved one

- Developing a memorial ritual for your loved one on special days or whenever you wish

Here are some examples and tips that may help people mourn and process their grief when they aren't able to be physically present with their loved ones, or when circumstances such as COVID-19, a global pandemic that required physically distancing occurs.

Tips for how people can mourn and process their grief while we are not able to gather:

Personal and collective rituals- these can occur online to create a sense of community.

Use social media to feel connected- social media can be a wonderful way to memorialize and connect with family and friends near and afar. It is also important to be mindful of the how social media can negatively impact one's grieving process. See the chapter on Grief and social media for more insight.

Offline- calling one on the phone, using facetime and other video-based applications can be helpful.

It's okay to begin planning the in-person celebration of life even if we don't have a set date.

Online support groups- these are especially helpful when we can find support groups that have members with shared losses. For example, groups for parents who've lost a child but be more helpful than a general grief support group.

Online therapy- seeking therapy can be a helpful resource in times of grief. Therapy can provide a safe and supportive space to process the loss and work towards creating new meaning post loss.

Social support is still important even when cannot physically gather. Be creative in utilizing your support system.

Bearing witness as a form of grief might include:

Looking at photos or compiling a book of memories, messages, stories and lesson associated with the loss.

Write letters. Grieving people are often encouraged to write letters to their loved ones, to parts of their selves (who needs something), to their old job, their old home, etc.

Capture your history. It might be helpful to capture to grasp the reality of the loss by cataloging the history of a relationship or loved one's life. This can be helpful in expressing feelings related to the loss.

Expressive arts. Drawings, paintings, sculptures, can be helpful to express a story or re-write one's journey on loss. It can be especially helpful for individuals who struggle with finding words to express themselves.

Write a story. This story can serve a variety of purposes. We often use stories to help individuals envision a life post loss. It might include prompts such as Who am I know? What's different now? How are others doing?

Saying Goodbye. Some people may not have had an opportunity to say goodbye. This exercise can take place in a variety of formats include letter writing, "phone call", empty chair exercise and more. If one assumes that their loved one can hear them all they need is to start the conversation. This can be a powerful exercise for people navigating the grief journey.

Resource in the portal: Grief bibliotherapy, groups and other resources

Did you receive a nugget that helped you? Share with me if you feel moved at thegift@ajitarobinson.com

NOTES:

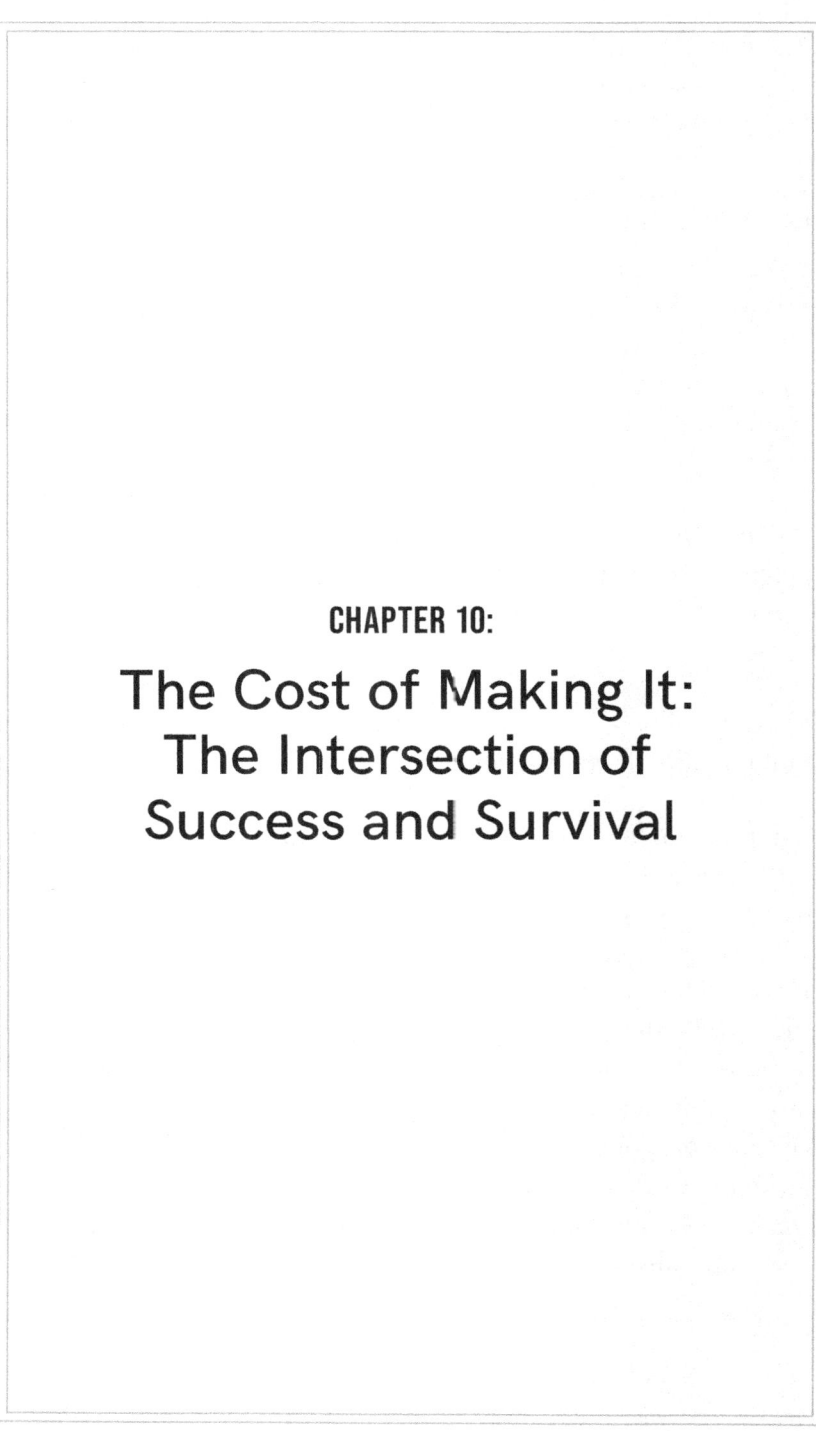

CHAPTER 10:

The Cost of Making It:
The Intersection of
Success and Survival

Striving to succeed often requires discipline, clarity, and perseverance. Oftentimes, there is a great deal of sacrifice. Many of us who are starting at "ground zero" are in survival mode on the path to success.

There is a cost associated with success and understanding it can help us pivot from surviving to thriving. This chapter will highlight the unique and unshared challenges that first-generation trauma survivors and first-generation poverty disruptors often encounter on their journey "of making it". This final chapter is a conversation about how this shift from survival to success impacts the individual, family dynamic and what we need to know to reclaim ourselves and more firmly navigate this part of the journey.

This is a discussion of symbolic and physical losses encountered by people who are taught through experience and socialization how to survive. This is a conversation for those who know what it is like to go without and to make something out of nothing.

For those of us who were taught to pay bills but were not taught to build wealth. This is for you.

For those of us who were taught to just work harder without acknowledging that our value exists in our being and not solely in our doing. This is for you.

There is a lot that we grieve as we navigate moving from survival to successfully thriving. We might find ourselves going back to spaces, using skills and narratives that we learned when we were in survival mode. This might be the first time you acknowledge all that you endured on your journey. One of the things that I talk about a lot in my work as a trauma and grief therapist is how to recognize when we are no longer in survival mode and when we no longer need the skills that we acquired during that time in our lives.

I call this, "identifying what armor we can put down." We might find ourselves being glorified as "survivors' but also feeling unseen because people might be encountering us at our "Chapter 10" and we look well-polished. I often tell people to not get stuck on the shiny nature of Chapter 10, doing so guarantees that we miss the road traveled and things endured to arrive to this place. To skip over the journey would be a mistake. To skip to the end and deny the path traveled prior to arriving to this place, a path that is filled with resilience, pain, and sacrifice would leave the story untold, unheard. The denial would be another loss on top a mountain of losses.

If you were to look at my chapter 10, you would note that I am a multiple 7-figure entrepreneur who owns multiple successful businesses. You would note that I have effectively interrupted the intergenerational transmission of trauma and poverty. I have created stability and wealth for my children. The legacy is alive and fulfilled in this very moment.

If you skip to Chapter 10, you would not see the young girl whose Adverse Childhood Experience (ACE) score was an 8 out of 10 before I reached 9 years of age. What you would not see is the parental incarceration, addiction to drugs and the physical and emotional abuse. You would not see the period in life where I had to decide between paying my light bill ($36) and buying a book in undergrad. What you would not see is the broken bone in my cheek, first fractured by a broom as a child and re-broken in adulthood by an abusive partner. You would miss all those things if you only focused on how you might encounter me today. These places I've been were important parts of my journey because they impacted the choices, I made along the way to survive. The fact that I have 2 Bachelors, 2 Masters and a doctorate and a host of certifications makes sense for a kid that learned at an incredibly young age that education was an opportunity to disrupt poverty. Education became a coping mechanism for a kid who went to school 6 days a week during high school and every summer to stay safe, to stay hidden, to stay away from a home that was unpredictable at best, and unsafe on days were alcohol was plentiful and the music was loud.

FINDING WAYS TO ESCAPE

Excelling academically became a lifeline, my identity. When I finished my doctoral program and checked all the boxes, I found myself lost, yet again. I had to grieve no longer being a student. I had to grieve not knowing who I was outside of being an achiever, a doer. At Chapter 10, I present very well. If you got stuck there, you would never force me to unpack the trauma of repeated abusive relationships or the fact that I became a caregiver at the age of 10 for the first time and nearly 25 years later I find myself as a long distanced caregiver yet again.

You would miss all the experiences where I sat at the intersection of success and survival if we only discuss where I am today. These are only some of the highlights of my story. I often give this overview when I start with a new therapist…to see if they can handle my kind of trauma…you know the kind that permeates through generations and changes your DNA. The kind that is ancestral, generational, historical, and political.

If you skip to chapter 10, you run the risk of your of leaving those you encounter feeling disenfranchised, feeling unseen and unheard…and unable to unpack the chapters that precede the open page before you…with armor acquired along the way…armor that is far too heavy to keep holding. You would miss the opportunity to bear witness to the healing that comes with unpacking, rewriting the narrative and embarking on a road less traveled.

Part of this unpacking requires that we learn to identify when we are safe. When we no longer have to operate from a place of survival. When we can thrive. For many of the people who have a similar story, remnants of poverty, cumulative trauma, being in a world that dishonors Blackness, they might tell you that hyper productivity is a trauma response… and that doing is a form of survival.

So, I checked all the boxes, got all the degrees, did all the work (harder), worked all the jobs (better), saved money like it might never return, because I knew what it meant to be poor and I couldn't do that for the rest of my life. That looked like success. But it was survival.

I had to find a way to learn to live from a place of abundance, to embrace that I deserved to live fully in chapter 10 and be in a thriving space and not in survival. This required that I unpack my trauma so that I could grieve all that I endured and to unpack the notion that what my 9-year-old self-needed was never within reach. I want to invite you on this journey to explore the collective narratives I have had the privilege of witnesses over my life (personal experience) and career working as a trauma disruptor and first-generation poverty disruptor. It took me years to realize, I spent half my career learning to be who I needed as a child. On the other side, its an honor to work with those who I am invited to bear witness to their journey towards thriving.

I hope that you treat this discussion as an offering from those who were the first: the first to go to college, the first to make it out < place, thing, circumstance>, the first to disrupt addiction, the first to build our way out of poverty.

The first of many that often leaves us with a journey that is unique, navigators of paths unknown. Being the first on an unpaved journey is unique in that there is often no guide that is accessible, that is within our reach. Those of us who understand trauma knows that at the core of trauma is a loss of safety, a feeling that many of us embarking on things on our own experience on this journey. Even when we have family systems that are supportive of our endeavors, we may not have the language, or we may not have guides who have been where we are going. The cost of being the first means that we make mistakes and endure the costs financially, emotionally, and psychologically of not knowing. This unique and unshared journey can create a disproportionate experience and disproportionate load across the lifespan for first generation folks.

DEFINING SUCCESS

Webster's dictionary defines success as "the accomplishment of an aim or a purpose." For first generation people we may need to expand our thoughts about success and understand that for those in survival mode, success might be more aligned with Maslow's hierarchy of needs. For someone navigating trauma success may sound like: "I just want to stay safe today", "I just want to learn how to be invisible so that I'm out of harm's way", "I want to get to a place where I don't have to choose between basic necessities". Achieving these things is not defined or coded as success. It is survival.

The other interesting piece that I think is important about language in the storytelling aspect of this journey is that many of those who you will encounter may not describe their experience as trauma. I did not learn that I had a traumatic childhood until I was an adult. I began to realize that there was something different about my experiences, about my household, but I did not have any other point of reference. I had limited exposure to what healthy family dynamics looked like so my idea of normal and "success" was defined based on what I was repeatedly exposed to: poverty, drugs, abuse, addiction. I learned what I did not want far sooner than I learned what I desired. This created a pattern of operating out of "deficit" instead of abundance. I made decisions based on the absence of pain without properly screening for the presence of peace, happiness, and joy.

THE COST OF BEING THE FIRST

Being the first to go to college, launch a business, break the generational curses, whatever the pattern is comes with costs that we aren't often prepared for and with losses we rarely have an opportunity to name and grieve.

Pursuing higher education and entering a job in Corporate American meant that I had to assimilate to navigate predominantly white spaces.

Even when our families desire to be supportive they may be limited in resources, knowledge, and social capital. You do not know what you do not know, which means we may not know how to navigate the different systems and structures. Our educational systems are elitist and can create a lifelong financial burden for first generation college students and graduates. These social, cultural, and financial gaps widen as we become burdened with debt and gap in earning potential which can negatively impact our ability to generate wealth and have disposable income.

"Jesus does not want me to be poor my whole life. I was poor in money but rich in faith. Now, I get to claim an abundance of both."
– Dr. Ajita M. Robinson

On this path to making it, someone should have said "Ajita, your quality of life sucks." There was no downtime. I was in survival mode, so I kept saying, "you just have to do this for four and a half years". I learned that I could not leave things up to chance. If I did not know what was going to happen, I was more open and vulnerable to being abused or being hurt.

I took these same childhood skills of survival and leveraged them to finish a doctoral program in 4 years instead of the normal 7 years. I had mapped out how I was going to do it in four and a half years in my very first semester. I studied the course catalogs, I went to office hours when I could, I looked up everything I could and developed a plan. For many, they hear this and they are impressed. It is impressive. It was also about control and having learned that I could only rely on myself to get things done. This is trauma. It becomes a part of you in a way that you cannot distinguish whether this is naturally who you are or who you had to be.

You know: Type A, Planner, Perfectionist, Overachiever, Hyper-productive. Trauma.

I did not plan to have any friends or a dating life, because I did not have time. The cost of getting distracted meant I would have to go back home; it would mean that I had failed, and I would repeat the cycle that generations before me had repeated. The cost was too great.

We learn to navigate these educational settings and workplaces all while understanding that we do not fully speak or understand the language. I don't mean English but rather the unspoken cultural ways of being that you learn through social cues or if someone puts "you on". The ways social networking and social equity is leveraged through generations that often is not capital Black and Indigenous People of Color have.

Even as we achieve success in these spaces, we learn that we are still minorities operating in spaces that weren't designed for us. Many of us learn how to create collectives, communities of advocates who will rally on our behalf, who speak a language we are not privy to.

LOSING HOME

Sometimes success creates a loss of "home" for first generation disruptors. We may no longer fully "fit" in our family of origin because of how far we've traveled but we also don't "fit" amongst our peers. This can create a sense of loss that we have to actively address to find our people. This journey to making it might feel like shedding our roots so that we can more fully become our unburdened selves. We have learned to survive. Surviving to a disruptor is being able to re-tell our story in a way that is no longer past-oriented. What we are tasked with doing is carrying the weight that shows up on this journey of making it and finding a space to set it aside. We often find ourselves sandwiched between the generation that preceded us and the one that we created. We are more likely to be parents, caregivers (emotionally, physically, and financially) than our peers. We are less likely to seek help. This collective weight combined with limited access to culturally safe healing spaces increases our health disparities.

We cannot afford to be sick or take time off from work because too many people depend on us to show up. We are socialized to disregard our own needs, to be disconnected from our bodies so that we can continue to produce. We go to work when we are sick, we care for our family when we are depleted, and we are praised for being committed and consistent. We are praised to continue to produce despite our own pain and suffering. We learn to deny the signals our body is sending us that we are approaching deprivation.

We lose ourselves on a quest to find a place of belonging, a home.

SEEKING HELP. BUILDING COMMUNITY

Resources that are crucial to have on the journey include: financial resources and literacy, emotional support, community.

Part of the healing work requires that we name our losses so that we can grieve. The physical losses and symbolic losses. The loss of knowing what we needed was out of our reach. The loss of a guide, of support, of safe spaces. The loss of stability, financial freedom, the way we lost ourselves along the way.

Healing requires that we might find a way to accept that service to others does not require self-sacrifice. We might understand that we do not have to say "yes", every time someone needs us. It is okay to say no without feeling like we are abandoning those we love and care for. Success on the other side of survival means not giving so much of yourself away that you do not have anything left. Success means fully centering yourself in your own life and not making deficit-based decisions.

Give yourself permission to rest on purpose. Serve from your overflow, and always fill your cup first.

Say it with me: I have done enough. I am enough.

Resource: Fireside chat with Dr. Ajita Robinson

Did you receive a nugget that helped you? Share with me if you feel moved at thegift@ajitarobinson.com

NOTES:

Made in the USA
Las Vegas, NV
08 July 2024

92027282R00080